PRAISE FOR "COMM

110659842

"Gordon's name is on a very short list ____ _____ lighthouses for me at critical times in my ___. I value Gordon's wisdom and honesty and I think that scores of other people will find the same hopeful teaching I found."

Jon Acuff,
Best-selling author of *Stuff Christians Like*

"I am grateful for this book. *Common Ground* will take you where other books on marriage leave off – it will honor the depth of your heart, and your own personal struggle to love your spouse in the way your heart wants. *Common Ground* will give the story of your marriage a place to land, in the bigger story of what God is trying to give you through the struggles in your marriage. Don't read this book if you don't want more of God and God's beauty. But read it, please read it, if you want to learn to love."

Jan Meyers Proett,
Counselor, speaker, author of *The Allure of Hope* and *Listening to Love*

"Can a book restore or strengthen a marriage? Of course not. Only God can. But *Common Ground* is a book God can use. Gordon tackles tough issues with soundly biblical creativity, practical wisdom, personal integrity, and fresh insights that provide real guidance. I don't think Satan likes this book. I know God does. This book deserves wide exposure."

Larry Crabb,
Best-selling author, psychologist and pioneer in Christian counseling

"Marriage is often recognized as a battlefield, but this book calls us to recognize that the greatest enemy is not our spouse, but evil. A wedding is a gateway into cosmic conflict with dark forces… and it is so easy to partner unknowingly with evil rather than with each other.

Writing with the wisdom of a professional counselor but from the vulnerable perspective of a flawed husband trying to get it right, Dr. Bals offers redemptive pathways that confront couples with the grace and strength of Christ, the One who will leads us from the embattled trenches to Common Ground."

Andrew Byers,
Author of *Faith Without Illusions: Following Jesus as a Cynic-Saint*

"Books on marriage are very numerous, but really good books on marriage are quite rare. This is a really good book! Couples will surely benefit by reading it. By practicing its truths they may enjoy much-needed growth and healing in their relationship. Highly recommended."

John H. Armstrong,
President, ACT 3 (Carol Stream, IL)

COMMON GROUND

GROUND

God's Gift of a Restored Marriage

COMMON GROUND

God's Gift of a Restored Marriage

By Dr. Gordon C. Bals
with Jodi MacNeal

DAYMARK
PRESS
www.daymarkcounseling.com

Ordering Information: Quantity sales. Discounts are available on quantity purchases. For details, contact the publisher at the address above or at (205) 871-3332.

Printed in the United States of America

Unless otherwise indicated, all Scripture quotations are taken from *The Holy Bible, New Living Translation*, Copyright © 1996, 2004, 2007 by Tyndale House Foundation. Used by permission of Tyndale House Publishers, Inc., Carol Stream, Illinois 60188. All rights reserved.

Scripture quotations marked NIV are from *The Holy Bible, New International Version®*, NIV®, Copyright © 1973, 1978, 1984, 2011 by Biblica, Inc.™ Used by permission. All rights reserved worldwide.

Scripture quotations marked ESV are from *The Holy Bible, English Standard Version®*, ESV®, Copyright © 2001 by Crossway, a publishing ministry of Good News Publishers. Used by permission. All rights reserved.

Scripture quotations marked MSG are taken from *The Message* by Eugene H. Peterson. Copyright © 1993, 1994, 1995, 1996, 2000, 2001, 2002. Used by permission of NavPress Publishing Group.

Cover design by Rob Barge, Hardware Graphic Design & Illustration
Cover photograph © by William Leonard. All rights reserved.
Author photographs by Andrea Graeve. All rights reserved.
Art direction by Jodi MacNeal

Publisher's Cataloging-in-Publication data

Bals, Gordon C.
    Common ground : God's gift of a restored marriage / by Dr. Gordon C. Bals;
        with Jodi MacNeal.
        p. cm.
    ISBN 978-0-9883283-0-3
    Contains bibliographical references.
        1. Marriage --Religious aspects --Christianity. 2. Marriage --Biblical teaching. 3. Families --Biblical teaching. I. MacNeal, Jodi. II. Title.
    BV835 .B325 2012
    248.8/44 –dc23

This book is dedicated to my wife, Dawn…
"My best friend, the one I laugh with, live for and love."

TABLE OF CONTENTS

PART 1

PART II

PART I

INTRODUCTION

My wife and I fell in love during an idyllic three months aboard ship. It was a perfect time – with as perfect a woman – as I ever could have imagined. So you wouldn't think that just a little more than a year later, I'd decide to pick a fight with my beautiful bride. *During our wedding.*

Dawn and I met doing missions training on a 500-foot ship called *Anastasis*, docked in Jamaica after Hurricane Hugo. On weekday mornings we took part in a discipleship training class, sharing the experience of learning and growing in our faith. On weekends we went to the beach or sightseeing and at night we hung out with the other students, playing games and having fun. They were the most captivating three months of my life.

I hadn't dated much at all during the seven years prior to meeting Dawn. I'd been broken and afraid and closed off in places I couldn't recognize. Falling in love with her began piercing the hardness stored in my heart. Dawn and I got lost in telling each other the stories of our lives, our families, our friends. I was captured by her fun-loving personality and felt like I was walking three feet off the ground whenever I was near her.

Near the end of the three months, I remember standing on the deck with Dawn. The ocean lapped gently against the ship, the sun was setting, and Dawn's hair blew lightly in the wind as I whispered to her, "You are so beautiful." In that moment I felt deeply touched by Dawn and the gift she was becoming to me. The connection, hope and beauty of that moment penetrated every part of my being.

Sixteen months later, as I stood in the front of the church waiting for Dawn and her father to walk down the aisle, I couldn't have been in a different frame of mind. I was furious.

A half-hour before the ceremony, one of my groomsmen had come to me with a piece of news that sent me into a tailspin. Ready for it? Dawn had unpacked her car.

Big deal, right? But I lost it. Completely. You see, we'd already filled her car to the brim with our belongings, planning to drive north for our honeymoon and continue to our new home. Somehow, through some unusual and chaotic circumstances, Dawn had unloaded everything. Now, after our evening wedding and reception, we needed to go back to her parents' house and repack the stupid car – not something any groom dreams of doing on his wedding night.

So there I was, minutes before our wedding was to begin, and I just came unglued. I tried to pray with friends, but none of our prayers could calm my agitation, my reeling thoughts or my anger. Several difficult aspects of the wedding weekend had contributed to the tension I'd already been feeling, but it was that unpacked car that pushed me over the edge. In ways I only see now because I have more wisdom, something was working to cause division in the very first hour of our married life together and I felt powerless to stop it.

Before very long, the ceremony started and Dawn began her walk down the aisle. She was beautiful beyond words, but I was too upset to savor the moment.

Now, other guys might have been able to wait until they'd gotten through the wedding and out of the church before picking a fight with their brand-new wives. Most guys, maybe, but not me. I jumped at the first chance I got – as we were kneeling together after taking communion. *During the ceremony.* Dawn just looked at me and smiled. I'll never forget her words, which were so much more forgiving and good-natured than I deserved: "I really don't think this is the time."

There, in our very first moments as husband and wife, an enemy of God was working to divide us. I couldn't hear or see the Lord telling me to relax and savor the moment. It was a foreshadowing of the division that would plague us for many years — a division that we lacked the maturity to resist together. Dawn was winsome and carefree and a heck of a lot more relaxed than me. I was uptight and unsure, and I'd been wrestling for months – years, really – with doubts about whether I could ever be a good husband.

Dawn and I had no idea that when we took our vows, we were entering a new form of spiritual warfare. In my marital counseling practice, I've seen this again and again. Two people fall in love and begin dreaming of a lifelong friendship that will provide comfort all their days. In the moments of infatuation, couples don't picture tension or angry words or the nights one of them will spend sleeping on the couch.

In the marriages I've seen as a counselor, the division and disorder don't come from couples' lack of effort or concern for each other. The vast majority of couples I've counseled have tried to integrate their Christian faith into their relationship and have worked to create a better marriage. Still, the ongoing tension remains. Why? What's the missing piece of the puzzle?

Evil.

The longer I read and meditated on the Scriptures, and the longer I practiced marital counseling, the more I began to see how much of the disconnection between couples was inspired by evil. Dawn and I had been unaware of this in our own marriage. So were the couples I counseled. Everywhere I looked, couples were blindly following evil into division.

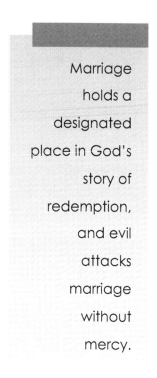

Marriage holds a designated place in God's story of redemption, and evil attacks marriage without mercy.

Over time, I sensed the Lord awakening me to the destructive work of evil in marriage and calling me to address it with the couples I was counseling. As those couples became more aware of evil and learned to follow and depend on the Lord as a way to disarm it, they began changing. Their marriages got better – yet they were expending less effort. As I helped them cooperate with God, they began to listen to Him and to rely on Him in a different way, and evil began to have less and less influence in their marriages. Because of their newfound insight and trust in God's ways, they began experiencing rest and togetherness, and didn't have to work so hard to achieve it.

Here's what I've come to know: Marriage holds a designated place in God's story of redemption. Evil loves divorce or division in marriage because God loves marriage and the redemptive love it builds in those who become lifelong friends. Make no mistake – evil attacks marriage without mercy. You have absolutely no idea what battle you're getting into when you say, "I do." At that point the evil one says, "Oh, really. You do? You really think you can be faithful to God, your spouse and your promises? We'll just see how faithful you can be. I will do everything I can to make a mockery of your marriage and God."

In this book, you'll uncover the lies that evil tries to plant within marriages. In place of such deceit I want you to hear God's truth, which can refresh your fatigue and strengthen your weakness. *God's heart is to take the brokenness you bring into marriage and the sin you perpetrate against one another and weave it into forgiving love.* This is God's redemptive story. Christ's death freed you from sin and evil and, through Him, God pursues you and can restore you into a more loving person. He wants to do this for you not because you try hard, but because He is kind.

The reason you are not to take your marital vows lightly is because God does not take them lightly. God was there the day you made them. Though you could not have understood fully the vows you made, He did. And this is how He responded: "Every day of your married life I will fight to bring you a better marriage. Your job is to learn how to look to Me and trust Me to let Me help you. When you said your vows, I knew you weren't really saying you would always do your best or try your hardest, because you won't. I know that. When you have stumbled and fallen in marriage, I will come to pick you up. Learn how to open your heart when I come to rescue you. That is your job in marriage. I want to redeem your brokenness and help you toward a more beautiful marriage. That was My vow to you on your wedding day."

1
COMMON GROUND:
WHAT IS IT, AND WHERE DO WE FIND IT?

You look at each other across the dinner table, and sometimes the distance may as well be 50 miles. Or 100. Or a million. And you wonder, "When did we stop being... together?"

It happens so easily and so often. When it does, couples don't always know how to react, what to do. A lot of them don't even know how to describe a strong marriage, let alone build one. Or they've tried everything they know to try, and still they feel an emptiness they don't know how to fill.

In nearly 20 years of counseling, I've met with hundreds of couples who each approach their marriage just a little differently. That's hundreds of styles of relating, but in all that time I've never met a husband and wife who were completely aware of how passionately God had promised to be involved in their marriage – or how incessantly evil would be fighting to destroy it.

I see well-meaning, hardworking people who've fallen into the trap of what I call the "Bootstraps Marriage." Here, couples face their struggles with genuine honesty, but believe the only solution is to fix the problems themselves – pull themselves up by their bootstraps. They identify their problems, talk about them, read books and attend seminars. They focus on what they can see – their problems and their effort. But no matter how hard they work, things don't improve dramatically.

Here's the flaw: When you accept a lie that says, "If you have marriage issues, you'd better get busy and solve them," you've actually moved away from disarming the problem. The energy behind the work is fueled by a belief that you are on your own when it comes to working out the problems.

Trying to pull a marriage up by its bootstraps wrongly inflates our own capabilities. We believe we're better than we can be. It diminishes the need for a larger wisdom and grace – God. It put the focus on working independently and it puts the solution in your grasp. It does not connect you to your need for Someone bigger than your spouse, your problems and your effort.

I sometimes see a very different situation – couples who believe they should be living their very own "Modern Romance." It's the type of marriage we read about in bestsellers and see in movies. There might be a challenge or two along the way, but in the end, the couple ends up happy and satisfied. If this is your prototype, I have upsetting news - it will actually make your marriage worse.

In a Modern Romance, you avoid your need for God's love and redemption. Why? Because you minimize the depth of pain in the marriage and you maintain a pretense of happiness. Over time, the energy it takes to pretend you have a good marriage, without addressing real hurts, will actually wear you out and cause your marriage to atrophy.

So much of the Christian literature about marriage either isn't honest enough about how intensely you really struggle or offers new forms of advice about how to work more diligently. When Christian counsel is used as a way to get people to pretend (the Modern Romance marriage) or to work harder (the Bootstraps Marriage), it's not appealing *or* helpful. Neither of these models defines marriage as the biblical drama it is. They fail to recognize the sinister nature of the problem (there's an evil one who hates God and everything He loves) and the profound beauty of the solution (God's love can redeem you and your marriage).

Perhaps you would be better served by another image, one that truly depicts your marriage as a difficult and major undertaking – spiritual, emotional and physical – that pushes you far beyond your own limits. When I first sit down with couples, I most often like to introduce the idea of climbing a mountain together as a way to describe their marriage. By its very nature, climbing a distant peak poses risk and danger, but also carries the promise of beauty and triumph.

This seems to resonate with people for several reasons. They seem to understand that there are common challenges each couple must work together to overcome, especially the unfamiliar terrain, the fierce storms, and the physical and emotional exhaustion. The elements represent the ways evil will assault you, and there will be many. Some, you'll recognize. Blistering cold, or wind so strong it will knock you off your feet unless you're roped together. Some will be more subtle, like the calm sunshine that lures you farther than it's safe to go.

You'd be foolish to journey onto the mountain alone. A climb this perilous demands the help and wisdom of a guide who knows every rock and outcrop and blade of grass on the mountain, who has a light for the dark places and a map to keep you from losing your way. Your guide will provide a tent and warm blankets when the snow flies, and lead you to cool, hidden springs when the sun feels merciless.

The difficulty of marriage is designed to force you to reach beyond yourself *toward Someone bigger.* You reach for God, your Guide, His wisdom revealed in the Scriptures, and His ministry through Jesus Christ. The counsel in Scripture brings you life when it is presented in a way that carries you through real difficulty.

MARRIAGE ISN'T EASY

One of the most repeated and simple lies evil throws at you as a couple is that your marriage shouldn't be hard – and that one (or both) of you is doing something wrong if it is. When I was a young husband, evil kept bullying me toward believing that my marriage should be easy and that other couples' lives were much more wonderful than ours. Those were lies. Every couple experiences heartbreak in their relationship, though it may or may not be reflected for the world to see. They may not even have grown the ability to see it for themselves. Maturing into the strength to submit to God's truth while resisting the onslaughts of evil took (and still takes) a lot of practice, a lot of humility, and a lot of courage.

What you can experience as a married couple are "tastes of heaven," moments in which you are refreshed together and reminded of why you are married. That's Common Ground.

Imagine yourselves partway up your mountain on your great climb, roped together but not entirely certain how helpful that really is. Your climbing ropes keep getting tangled, you can't always find the right pace, and you've disagreed about whose mountaineering skills are better. You round a rocky outcrop to discover a safe, sunny, sheltered ledge. Although there are miles left to go, here's a place you can take off your packs and rest, drinking in the view before you. Your Guide promised He'd lead you to this place of rest and awe, though you'd doubted it as you struggled. Now you're grateful and humbled.

At that moment, you both realize it would have been impossible to get to that point without each other. You value your relationship in a new way. You also experience a new bond with and respect for your Guide, and are prepared to listen to and follow Him more closely. Finally, the beauty that captures you from this new vantage point is breathtaking. You look back and can't believe you've come this far. It gives you hope and strength to journey a little farther up your mountain. In marriage, of course, we never truly reach the top. But I guarantee there are moments when you'll feel like you have.

> It's a thrill to discover the delights of the Lord's goodness and to live as though you hope for them.

There is much that's mysterious and beautiful about a Common Ground marriage. It's a thrill to discover the delights of the Lord's goodness, and to live as though you hope for them. What can *you* expect from a Common Ground marriage?

COMMON GROUND IS RESTFUL

The one aspect of finding Common Ground that has surprised me the most is how restful it is. Remember, the evil one does not want you to experience rest in your marriage. Evil loves chaos, drama and division. If you approach your marriage out of fear or responsibility, then the human desires that create unrest in marriage – hostility, quarreling, jealousy, outbursts of anger, selfish ambition, divisions

23

(Galatians 5:20) – will be intensified. Your marriage will have much more disarray than you want.

If you grow the ability to let God take your marriage on His back and then you learn to follow Him, the chaos of evil is quieted. As a result, the fruits of the spirit – love, joy, peace, patience, kindness, goodness, faithfulness, gentleness, and self-control (Galatians 5:22-23) – will be words that will more accurately depict the atmosphere around your marriage.

When you experience rest as a couple, and see what you are accomplishing together, you have tasted Common Ground. You enjoy and celebrate the sustenance and beauty that come from working together – and together with God – to disarm your enemy.

COMMON GROUND REQUIRES HUMILITY

I remember one Saturday morning about three months after our wedding, when I grabbed the car keys, said a quick goodbye to Dawn and headed out to run a quick errand. It took 20 minutes, and it was so insignificant I can't remember now what I went to get. What I *can* remember is that when I got home, Dawn was crying… because I hadn't asked her to come with me. This unnerved me, and I reacted. For the first time in our marriage I raised my voice at Dawn, which frightened her and made her cry even harder.

Instead of demonstrating what good and loving people we were, our marriage was actually revealing flaws we'd never recognized in each other or in ourselves. In his book *The Mystery of Marriage*, Mike Mason writes, "One of the hardest things in marriage is the feeling of being watched. It is the constant surveillance that can get to one, that can wear one down like a bright light shining in the eyes, and that leads inevitably to the crumbling of all defenses, all facades, all the customary shams and masquerades of the personality." As Dawn and

I tried harder to love one another, it seemed we grew farther apart. Efforts at disciplined work on the marriage made us more tense and demanding. Over time, the good marriage we'd hoped for seemed to be drifting slowly out of our reach. We were regularly overcome with despair. *This was part of God's plan. He needed us to accept how utterly incapable we were of producing genuine love so that when it finally emerged, He got the credit.*

As I look back, I realize that the humility we were developing in the first years of our marriage was crucial. It's what helped us turn to and listen to the Lord. Because our marriage was so far from perfect, the togetherness we'd eventually begin to enjoy was a tangible reminder that every good thing we receive on this earth comes as a gift from God (James 1:17). We learned to feel profoundly grateful in those moments when we could see that we were surrounded by His work, and not ours.

COMMON GROUND CELEBRATES KINDNESS

The humility you learn in marriage softens your hearts and allows for the possibility of growing into the biblical love Paul describes in 1 Corinthians 13. Such love is kind and unselfish, forgiving and merciful, strong and enduring. Your human nature will fight you on this, but only as your inner self is transformed will you be able to move toward genuinely loving each other.

For instance, I used to be extraordinarily attached to organization and neatness. It was just part of me. I couldn't stand for anything to be out of place. I'd sweep through our house, irritated, picking things up and putting them away. Deeply convicted of my anger, I prayed, "Lord, help me love Dawn whether or not she is ever neat like me." I believe I wanted to love her genuinely and kindly and patiently, but it's taken time for me to be transformed into that husband – much longer than I ever imagined.

It takes maturity in the Gospel to see and meet another person's need unselfishly, much as it does to receive such kindness humbly. As Dawn and I become kinder to one another, we demonstrate to each other the power of the resurrection and the work of Jesus in our lives to make us more like Him. As we awake to God's redeeming presence in our marriage, it helps us scoff at evil's work, past and present. By being more loving, we celebrate God's ability to work all things together for good.

COMMON GROUND OFFERS GLIMPSES OF HEAVEN

The gift of Common Ground lifts your marriage above evil. In those moments it becomes clearer that through marriage, you are participating intimately in the building of God's Kingdom and He is in your midst working it out. Your marriage is part of a larger story, and the redemptive togetherness you experience will transport you to a reality beyond this time on earth. Psalm 16:11 promises, "You will show me the way of life, granting me the joy of your presence and the pleasures of living with you forever."

Common Ground has a certain atmosphere. It is laced with gratitude, because you and your spouse recognize God as the author of your togetherness. It is humbling, because the struggles you face in your marriage reveal how incapable you are of producing what you want. It is kind, because God has used your marriage to soften your hardness and help you come together. It is celebratory, because you will recognize your triumph over evil. It is hopeful, because you realize your little moment is a foretaste of future glory. Common Ground is a gift, one that helps you stand above evil and realize that God's Kingdom is coming and will one day be here in fullness.

Through these tastes of heaven, you will be truly refreshed together and reminded of why you are married. They help you keep journeying through the difficulties you'll continue to have, no matter how much you learn or how much you change.

DAWN AND I REACH COMMON GROUND

To help you understand what I mean, let me tell you a story about a time Dawn and I experienced Common Ground in an overwhelming way, along with some history to show how much we've grown and changed with God as our Guide.

We'd left our three daughters with friends and were heading off on a weekend trip to celebrate our 16th anniversary. Not long into the drive, Dawn noticed a problem with our car. I was struck by how casually she mentioned it. You see, in the past she'd have been really afraid to tell me something was wrong, because I tended to get really defensive, really fast. In fact, she might not have said anything at all. Then, if the car eventually broke down (which it did), she would have felt even worse. She would have retreated into silence, and I would have spent most of our anniversary weekend pestering her to talk to me – not because I really cared about her, but because I knew the distance between us felt bad and I didn't want to feel bad.

But this time, it didn't go like that. Dawn mentioned the car didn't feel quite right, and I calmly wondered whether the front passenger tire had a bubble in it. (A couple weeks before our trip, Dawn had run over a pothole and bent the rim. We'd put on the full spare and were still riding on it.) It would have been like me to point out that the problem was *her* fault because *she'd* hit the pothole to begin with. But I didn't.

About 45 minutes later, Dawn told me the handling was getting worse. Normally, this second mention really would have irritated me.

For so much of my life I had been a man on guard, someone who was watching, working and moving to take care of my responsibilities and cover my bases. If someone close to me suggested I hadn't done my part or had failed to address something, I got agitated. I would have been thinking, "I heard you the first time and have been monitoring the situation. There was no need to remind me. Now you are going to pay for failing to trust my infinite capabilities." I probably would have gotten angrier and then sullen, stubbornly deciding we would ride on that tire until Kingdom come.

But this time, I surprised both of us by saying we'd pull over at our first opportunity. It occurred to me that I was different, by actually listening to Dawn and responding to what she said without being defensive. I also reasonably concluded that there was no reason to drive around all weekend with a bad tire. We even started playfully remembering our honeymoon, when our car broke down three times.

Several minutes later the tire blew, so I pulled off to a flat spot where I could change it. Though I am mechanically challenged, I soon had the van jacked up and the lug nuts off. I yanked as hard as I safely could, but I could not get that tire to budge. So I decided let our auto club finish the job.

Before I could make the call, though, a good-natured farmer type pulled over to help. He smiled and told me, "All you gotta do is kick it." With one swift kick of his cowboy boot, the bad tire was loose and we were back in business. I finished the job and we were on the road in minutes.

In the past, getting schooled by a pickup-driving good ol' boy would have killed any hope for a fun weekend. Convinced my masculinity had suffered one assault after another, I would have gone into some self-pitying funk while Dawn continued to shrink away from me. Yet, amazingly, we laughed about it all and continued on our way. *It was becoming clear that we weren't just celebrating a date on the calendar, but celebrating the many changes in the way we treated one another.* It was the best time we'd had together in years.

On the way home I brought up how well I thought things had gone on our trip. I'd actually resisted the urge to mention this before; Dawn isn't wild about my constant need to analyze our relationship. So, when I finally said something – and patted myself on the back for holding my tongue that long – she laughed, knowing how long I'd struggled to restrain myself. Her laughter in that moment only added to the beauty of the weekend.

The story could end there, and I'd still be able to call it a celebration of Common Ground. But it doesn't. After we got home, our three young daughters brought out a large wrapped package. Dawn opened it to find an anniversary book that our girls, aged 11, 9 and 7, had been working on for three months. They told us, "Even though we kept fighting, we stayed at it." It not only surprised us, but it answered some questions; during our weekend away, we'd even talked about how much closer our girls seemed lately.

The book was more than 30 pages long. Our older daughters, Aimee and Abby, let their youngest sister, Elise, make a couple of pages by herself. We'd continually tried to teach our daughters that you display true character when you protect and nurture the weakest among you. Now we saw the fruit of those words.

There was a page of memories and a page showing what they loved about Mom and Dad. There was a page called "Sisterhood." Aimee drew a picture of herself and her sisters at a carnival, the three of them standing on a "nurture scale" with the recorded measurement shooting out the top. In the surrounding crowd, one person was saying, "Boy, their parents must be great!" Elise had put together a bunch of pictures of our family life – each of which included her – and we all laughed about that.

Then, Dawn and I were officially invited to the debut performance of something called "Sisters in Motion," though we weren't sure just what that meant. We walked downstairs into our finished basement, which has three closets. Each daughter got into a closet, and music began to play. All at once they emerged and performed a choreographed dance to *Because You Live*, a teeny-bopper version of a song about gratefulness. The choreography was creative and the girls moved in perfect sync. I wondered, "Who taught them these moves and made them practice?" I was overwhelmed when they told us they'd devised everything – including the book – all by themselves.

Afterward, we all sat on the couch together and talked about the evening. Aimee said, "Dad, I've seen you cry before, but I have never seen you cry like that." She was right. After a few minutes, Dawn noticed it was the girls' bedtime. But I said, "No, I have never felt this close to heaven. This celebration can't end. Let's go out for ice cream!" And we did.

Compared to the anger I felt during our wedding ceremony, the anniversary weekend with Dawn and the gifts from our girls felt like reaching that beautiful, unexpected sunny spot on the side of our mountain. We stopped in a peaceful place for a time, finding ourselves stunned by all the beauty surrounding us. I had no idea I was headed for such beauty when Dawn and I had begun our walk together 16 years earlier.

I'd started off marriage very afraid, having no idea how much I was going to need a guide, how many treacherous passages we would need to pass through, and how much I would need to celebrate little victories along the way. I was too immature and fearful to experience true togetherness with my wife on our wedding day. Sixteen years later, I found it with my wife and our daughters for one simple reason: Jesus Christ.

ONLY CHRIST CAN CREATE COMMON GROUND

In marriage, you are empowered to "submit to one another *out of reverence for Christ,*" (Ephesians 5:21). My ability to move through my anxiety, fear and anger and give myself to my wife changed and grew as I got to know the Lord better. Along the way I began to realize that when I fell short in loving Dawn, it was an opportunity to trust the Lord to do something I couldn't see and didn't deserve. As I grew the humility to experience His forgiveness, let Him help me and see the wisdom in His guidance, I became a better husband.

When Dawn and I found ourselves in places that surprised us or seemed better than we deserved, we began to recognize God's kindness. I've written about how a mountain climbing guide can help you navigate dangerous passages, reveal your great capacity to overcome, and encourage you along the way. But the gratitude you'd show a guide can't compare to what I have felt toward the Lord as our marriage has reached places we couldn't have approached on our own.

In Colossians, Paul says that Christ's life in us is our hope of glory (1:27). One of the reasons I know this is true is that I so often wanted to quit, to run away from Dawn, but something inside compelled me to stay and keep trying. Through difficulty and pain, Christ came alive in me. He stood up inside of me and kept pursuing my wife through me while I hung on for dear life. When I reminisce about where we are in marriage, I don't feel an ounce of pride. I'm simply grateful that Jesus' love has been stronger than the unbelief I often display.

In our life together, there have been so many moments where evil robbed, killed and destroyed the glory God was growing in our marriage. But for us, the splendor of our anniversary weekend was so vast that it helped me grab hold of God's sovereign care to see the ways our marriage was growing and how we were coming together.

The greatest gift of our marriage is that it has helped us to look beyond ourselves for the Lord. Our marriage is a continual reminder that out of reverence for Him, we submit or give ourselves to each other. He has been the author of our oneness.

EVIL: NOT EVERYBODY'S HAPPY ABOUT YOUR MARRIAGE

I've discovered that believers spend very little time discussing evil and the way it deviously and mercilessly attacks marriage. That's perfectly understandable – most times, it's not even on their radar. But we need to be aware and alert. Scripture warns us that "the world around us is under the power and control of the evil one," (1 John 5:19). When you consider how relatively few marriages flourish, it becomes easier to recognize Satan as the prince of this world. His deceit and division wreck way too many marriages, and he's rarely exposed for the culprit he is.

This is exactly how he wants it to be. He loves to deceive, and when people point fingers at one another without recognizing evil's influence, they play right into his scheme. His vile contempt is fueled by our naïveté; as husbands and wives cast blame on everything and everyone but him, evil is energized. "Evil is not simply the absence of good, nor is it merely erroneous choice. Evil is revolt, disobedience, resistance. It is a human (and demonic) refusal to carry out God's purposes in history," writes Robert Webber in *Who Gets to Narrate the World*? "It is a deliberate, intentional and violent rejection of God."

And it's not just Satan we're facing, either. In reality, three branches of evil work together to desecrate God's splendor. In *3 Crucial Questions about Spiritual Warfare*, Clinton E. Arnold observes, "The Bible teaches that there are three forms of evil influence that exert their power over the lives of people to lead them into transgression and away from God. These three enemies are simply described as the world, the flesh and the devil. In some passages of the Bible, one of these sources of evil influence might be discussed more than the other two, but in general, the Bible maintains a balance among these three evil influences." This has major implications for every relationship, because as evil works against marriages he positions himself to attack other cherished structures God adores – our families and His Church.

Children thrive in the soil of a good marriage. A sound, loving marriage creates an atmosphere that helps children see and hear God and grow more fluidly into life-giving adults. If a husband and wife grow in their faith, letting their marriage reveal (and then soften) their hard-heartedness, they become different people. They become more loving, wise, and unselfish. They are freer to give to their children and they don't demand that their kids come through for them. In short, a good marriage helps a husband and wife learn real love that they can, in turn, lavish upon their children.

Divided parents create an atmosphere that wounds the hearts of children and makes it harder for them to hear and respond to God. Accomplishing this, evil triumphs.

Likewise, evil has a vested interest in hobbling the Church. Clinton Arnold continues, "Satan and his forces fiercely pursue their objective of promulgating all forms of evil in the world. This includes, above all, deceiving people and hindering them from grasping the truth about God's revelation of himself in the Lord Jesus Christ. But it also includes working to bring about the demise of the Church through inciting more evils among its members."

The way a man cares for his wife will be a good indication of how he will care for God's people. If he cannot faithfully love his wife, then his ability to care for the people of God comes into question. If a wife is suffocating in her marriage, she will have a harder time being a life-giving part of the Church. I have seen this truth play out time and time again. So much of healthy church life hinges on relationships, and the vast majority of problems in a church body grow out of the brokenness of those relationships. Marriage can serve as a haven for men and women to be restored and healed relationally so they can in turn have more life to bring a church body. Instead, it seems marital problems end up carrying significant burdens into the lives of our churches.

In 1 Timothy 3, Paul says that all church leaders are to be faithful to their wives – and I don't believe this just means staying together. In essence, loving faithfulness in marriage is a measure for a man's fitness to be a caregiver in God's Church. If leaders were first changed by their marriages and restored by God, they would become men and women with the strength, discernment and tenderness to care for God's people. Thus, one way to shore up church life is to build redemptive marriages.

WHO EVIL MOCKS: JESUS

The hardened divisions that occur in so many marriages (we've come to know them as "irreconcilable differences") make a mockery of God's longing to build redemptive love. When a husband and wife display a pursuing, forgiving love, they show the world a transcendent picture of Christ's love for His Church. No wonder evil despises it so.

Here's what evil wants you to believe instead: That your spouse needs to be good enough to deserve your love. Instead of growing forgiveness, evil tries to pull you into feeling justified in withholding it. In fact, he's thrilled when the love between you is conditional.

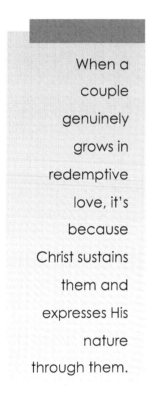

When a couple genuinely grows in redemptive love, it's because Christ sustains them and expresses His nature through them.

If I genuinely learn to love my wife the way the Bible defines love, then I have grown to the place where I give my wife a love that *she will never deserve.* I give her my love as a gift to help her hear and respond to Jesus and to become a better woman. In the same way, if she loves me with a redemptive love, it could never be something I have earned. My wife gives me her love as a gift to help me become a better man. We don't deserve the love we give each other, because it comes from a much bigger place than our humanity. If a couple genuinely grows in redemptive love, it will be because Christ sustained each spouse and expressed His nature through them.

Evil hates this. Evil will do what it can to keep you from enduring in your marriage so that you give up on redemptive love once and for all. If evil can separate you from God and from each other, then your hearts will remain hard and all those in the circle of your world will experience the loss. I cannot emphasize this enough. The evil one hates that Jesus died to set us free. The cross mocked evil and turned it upside down. Evil loves to ridicule Christ's sacrifice and make it as meaningless as possible in the life of every believer. When you love your spouse out of reverence for what Christ has done, you are saying, "Jesus is alive! *Jesus is alive!* He has set me free! Suffering and rejection don't own me in my marriage – Christ does!" Evil wants to own you by hardening you against redemptive love.

WHAT EVIL OFFERS: TEMPTATIONS OF THE FLESH

In his epistle, John writes: "Stop loving this evil world and all that it offers you, for when you love the world, you show that you do not have the love of the Father in you. For the world offers only the lust for physical pleasure, the lust for everything we see, and pride in our possessions. These are not from the Father. They are from this evil world," (1 John 2:15-16). It's especially helpful to focus on two words: lust and pride. They work together. *The beguiling nature of the world continually tries to pull you toward self-reliance and away from God.*

Sensual pleasure, material goods and independence tug at you. Evil will tell you that God's ways are not necessary as a foundation for your life; the world would like you to treat God as an accessory, at best. This is the lie. The world says, "God isn't that important. He doesn't really care about what you do. His Word? That's for other people. You're independent enough to know what's best. Take care of yourself." The world pulls at the cravings of your flesh, claims they're real and authentic, and promises to bring life apart from God. The world's temptations feed your pride to handle your destiny on your own.

The flesh is a treacherous presence that dwells inside every human being. It is evil. Remember, when we speak of the flesh, we're not referring to skin and bones but to the twisted and tangled desires of frail, weak human beings. "The sinful nature (flesh) is always hostile to God. It never did obey God's laws, and it never will," (Romans 8:7). In *The Enemy Within*, Kris Lundgaard explains,

"The flesh hates everything about God. Since it resists everything about God, it resists every way we try to taste him and know him and love him. And the more something enables us to find God and feast on him, the more violently the flesh fights against it."

As we'll explore in later chapters, God calls a husband to be steadfast, sacrificial and understanding, but a husband's flesh is double-minded, indifferent and antagonistic. God calls a wife to awe, cooperation and rest, but the flesh of a wife is resentful, callous, and hectic. Your flesh will always try to drag you away from your calling as a husband or wife, away from your spouse and away from your God. Evil depends upon this.

WHAT EVIL PRACTICES: TELLING LIES

Evil loves to assault you and inflame your flesh with lies. I really struggled with evil's lies during our ninth year of marriage. We had three little girls – none older than 4. We'd bought our first house, which needed repairs we couldn't pay for and weren't talented enough to do ourselves. I worked part-time at a young, struggling church and part-time as a counselor for the non-profit organization I was trying to get off the ground. I had just begun to pursue my doctorate. We were doing all of this on a ministry salary in a materialistic culture. I was overloaded with stress, my faith weak with fear and despair, and I was especially susceptible to the lies evil whispered in my ear.

He kept pointing out how unfairly God had treated me. He brought to mind other couples we knew, couples who were younger than us but had nicer homes and more money and no problem paying for a deck repair or a kitchen project, while we couldn't even replace our ancient windows. He pointed out families with relatives in town – built-in, free babysitters. (Dawn and I hardly ever got to go on a date together; for one of us to get some time away, it meant the other needed to stay home and watch the kids.) Although Dawn was working just as hard as I was, her faults and failures were plastered across my mind like billboards.

The evil one saw the frailty of my faith and regularly suggested three very unsettling messages: that God didn't care about me; that Dawn wasn't doing her part; and that I never should have married her. He wanted me to believe that almost any life – other than the one I was living – would provide the relief I needed. Evil was inflaming my flesh, trying to wear me down so I would abandon my marriage.

Evil tries to wear you down, so you will abandon your marriage.

In His great mercy, God revealed evil's lies and He preserved our marriage and my faith. Evil hadn't counted on how large the Lord was in my heart and how He was able to help me follow my love for Dawn and our girls. We had a strong circle of believing friends who surrounded us, and I had an inkling that God was calling me to endure through this season of intense discomfort and into something far more contented. One day we'd recognize that something as Common Ground.

You forget that evil pursues you with sweet-sounding lies composed just for your ears. The Bible says the evil one is "looking for some victim to devour," (1 Peter 5:8). The adulterous woman in Proverbs 9 represents evil's schemes: "The woman named Folly is loud and brash. She is ignorant and doesn't even know it. She sits on her doorway on the heights overlooking the city. She calls out to men going by who are minding their own business. 'Come home with me,' she urges the simple," (Proverbs 9:13-16). During my stressed-out, vulnerable time, though I was doing my best to stay focused on loving my wife and daughters and finding my place in ministry, tempting thoughts kept dogging me. I wasn't out looking for trouble, but it was looking for me.

WHAT EVIL LOVES: ANGER AND VENGEANCE

You are born into a world where you will suffer harm. As soon as possible, evil will try to make you believe this is because God is not concerned about you. This causes you to move out into the world to protect yourself, either lashing out or distancing yourself from others, whether you recognize it or not. You anticipate the damage others will do to you and you relate to the world in self-protective ways. This is the meaning of vengeance – returning an injury for an injury – and this style of relating grows as evil keeps whispering that you are alone and unprotected.

Through the flesh, evil arouses your vengeance toward God but pushes you to act it out on the people around you. Unbelief forms a firm foundation for vengeance, as evil keeps trying to get you to agree that God is holding out on you. You will injure, punish or demean yourself or others because this world is difficult and painful and does not consistently honor your deepest longings.

Let me give you a very simple example of what vengeance can look like in marriage, one I see all the time in my practice: Husband is late getting home from work, and wife is angry.

Here's one scenario: The wife got home from her job on time, served dinner to the kids and cleaned up. Just as she is about to sit down and rest, she gets a call from her husband, who is already running late. Again. "I'm going to be another 45 minutes," he tells her. She says goodbye, hangs up, and with one angry motion sweeps her husband's already-cold dinner into the trash. It's a simple act of vengeance. She makes her husband pay because he didn't come through for her.

Let's flip the outcome. Say the husband's really been trying to get home, but the demands of the day have just been piling up and piling up. He feels bad when he has to call to say he'll be another 45 minutes late. His wife reacts with impatience and frustration, and he lashes back, "OK, if you're going to be like that, I'll come home whenever I feel like it." He makes *her* pay. He eats his dinner in a restaurant and comes home after she's gone to bed. That is another simple act of vengeance.

Most couples I know don't think of themselves as vengeful people, and most likely they would not recognize how vengeance energizes their marital discord. Christians, especially, know that "anger gives a mighty foothold to the Devil," (Ephesians 4:27) so have become practiced – quite without realizing it – at being vengeful without ever acting angry.

Let me give you an example. A wife works extra-hard one day to get the kids ready for bed before her husband gets home. She's picked up his favorite meal, greets him at the door with a warm smile and a kiss, and tells him, "Tonight I want you to just relax. I really want you to do whatever you want." Her husband thanks her, sitting down at the table to eat as he answers e-mails on his phone. After ten minutes of watching his preoccupation, the wife leaves the table and goes into the other room to sulk. She didn't realize it, but vengeance had been motivating her all day. No, she hadn't spent the afternoon consciously recalling all the moments he'd neglected her over the past several weeks, but those moments were there with her all the same. Underneath her loving actions she was energized by this thought: "I'm going prove to my husband that he doesn't pursue me, doesn't care about me and doesn't love me." As he sits there busily checking e-mails, she's gotten the proof she was looking for. Because she *didn't* really want him to just rest and relax and do what he wanted. She wanted *him* to give *her* some attention, and when he doesn't, she punishes him – and herself.

Later that evening they discuss how much time he spends at the gym. Neither of them realizes the wife brought this up to condemn him for his selfishness. After she left the table, vengeance brought to her mind all the ways he chooses everything but her. As she agreed with it, she tried to bully her husband into submission by making him feel bad about the time he spends working out. He obviously became defensive and more hardened.

She feeds on anger that God "allowed" her to marry a man who lets her down, and she acts this out in the relationship. She's decided her husband shouldn't get anything he wants or needs until he learns to take care of her properly. Sadly, but not unexpectedly, her husband will do the same thing. In his mind, his wife's constant disappointment with him justifies his inattention to her needs. When she learns to be supportive, then he'll change toward her. What's amazing is that this couple would tell you they don't argue and are not vengeful. Can you see how they are both relational bullies, without ever raising their voices?

WHAT EVIL PROMOTES: DIVISION AND CHAOS

Vengeance fuels a fleshly contempt at God that can be intoxicating, pulling you into a pattern of divisive behavior before you realize it. I still forget that many of my choices to organize, work extra-hard, or avoid relaxing are energized by my perception that this world is not as safe as I want it to be. As I feed into the evil-inspired pull, I live in the flesh.

Because your flesh opposes God, it will pull you away from being accepting and forgiving of your spouse. After a husband spends the morning watching the news, his wife snaps at him when she gets home from spin class. She wishes he'd take better care of himself, and all during her class the voice of evil was inflaming her flesh, reminding her what a sedentary life her husband leads. Meanwhile, her husband can't understand why she seems to spend more and more time at the gym when he's home alone. Why can't they do something they'd both enjoy, he wonders, even if it's relaxing in front of the TV? Evil helps him convince himself she doesn't care anymore.

Every couple has regular points of disagreement that grow out of fleshly attachments. God created us differently to add shape and beauty to the world, but when we live in the flesh, we use those gifts selfishly and it fosters divisiveness in marriage.

Evil loves chaos. While I can be serious and driven, Dawn is funny and relational. I kept trying to get Dawn to join me on the path of discipline and she kept trying to help me enjoy life. I beat her up with organization and she shamed me with laughter. Our flesh incited a chaotic mess that we got lost in. When it came to confronting our fleshly way of living and growing a warm acceptance of each other, we often followed evil and ran the other way. I felt irresponsible if I laughed or enjoyed life and Dawn felt controlled and stifled if she organized or planned something. The lies we believed and trusted got in the way of our togetherness. Marriage was calling us to a deeper faith that required less attachment to our flesh, but we were too self-reliant. The evil one played on our vulnerability and immaturity and bullied us further into our flesh, where we could find a false sense of comfort and remain divided from each other and God.

For one couple it's a friction over money management. For another, it's constant disagreement over how to raise the children. When Dawn and I were falling in love our differences attracted us to one another, but after some years in marriage they began to challenge and divide us. We kept bullying each other without realizing we were just following our flesh.

Referring to the work of marriage researcher John Gottman, Dr. Fred Luskin writes in *Forgive for Love*, "One of his most provocative findings was that approximately 70 percent of the issues that couples disagree about at the beginning of the relationship do not change over time." *Seventy percent of the issues that couples disagree about at the beginning of the relationship do not change over time.* That is a powerful finding. Evil pulls us into ways of approaching life and relating that are hard to step out of. Couples fight the same fights their whole married life.

When the person you are married to hurts you over and over, the same way, for a lifetime, it becomes almost reflexive to make them pay in return. Dawn and I still let each other down in similar ways, but it is the growth and change that we celebrate. The work of the Gospel, God's good news, is slowly giving us freedom from the power of the flesh. The good news is that marriage is uniquely designed to help you see your flesh and step out of it – but only with the Lord's help.

CRACKING THE ENEMY'S CODE

I always thought the best part of marriage would be our romantic moments, and they have been richly beautiful. But I've found there is something even more powerful about working with the Lord to untangle the deceptive work of evil and setting back upon His path together.

Marriage is unlike any other relationship. It's not unusual to be unprepared for this. When we were a young couple, Dawn and I each approached marriage the same way we'd managed everything else in our lives. I believed in hard work and discipline. Dawn thought we needed more laughter, and that relaxation would be our salvation. I worked more because Dawn relaxed more; Dawn relaxed more because I worked harder. *Who can help you see your commitment to fleshly living mostly clearly? Many times it's the one you blame it on – your husband or your wife.*

Sadly, and this is true for most people, I only began to see the foolishness in my fleshly living because of the way Dawn and I were hurting each other. I became depressed and she began to wither in our marriage. The closeness and consistency of marriage brought us face-to-face with a reality we couldn't ignore. We did not love like God. We could not tolerate being hurt and couldn't love when we felt disappointment. Long after we started hurting each other, we began to recognize the difference between the way we loved each other and what God was calling us toward. Finally, we started to cry out to the Lord for change. It was a gift we needed.

"To put it simply, marriage is a relationship far more engrossing than we want it to be," Mike Mason writes in *The Mystery of Marriage*. "It always turns out to be more than we bargained for... Only marriage urges us into these deep and unknown waters. For that is its very purpose: to get us out beyond our depth, out of the shallows of our own secure egocentricity and into the dangerous and unpredictable depths of a real and interpersonal encounter."

Eventually I began to understand how many of my patterns were intended as strategies to avoid disappointment. You become committed to rebellion because you keep listening to the voice of evil, which tells you love should never hurt. Sure, my approach to life helped me escape rejection and disappointment in sports and school when I was a child and in work as an adult. But the longer I stayed married, the more I saw there was no way to run away from disappointment. I hadn't realized that I'd entered marriage believing not only that love should never be painful, but if it was, then surely God was holding out on me. Thus, I was living to stay one step ahead of the discomfort that would surely come. The gift of marriage is that it exposes how hard you try to avoid pain in the way you love.

C.S. Lewis says it well in *The Four Loves*, his wise reflection on our capacity to experience and share this tender, powerful emotion: "To love at all is to be vulnerable. Love anything, and your heart will certainly be wrung and possibly be broken. If you want to make sure of keeping it intact, you must give your heart to no one, not even to an animal... We shall draw nearer to God, not by trying to avoid sufferings inherent in all loves, but by accepting them and offering them to Him; throwing away all defensive armour."

When you follow vengeance into fleshly living, you have neither the awareness nor the energy to address the real wrongs in a relationship. You don't understand that you can't avoid disappointment at all; at best, it can serve a redemptive purpose. As psychotherapist and teacher John Welwood notes in his book *Journey of the Heart*, "How we relate to love's pain ... can lead in one of two very different directions. If we regard it as a threat, something to avoid at all cost, we will try to patch it over, keep it out of sight. [Remember the Modern Romance marriage?] After a while, however, accumulating patches only deadens our sensitivity and our capacity to love freely. Resenting the pain involved in becoming vulnerable to another person

> The gift of marriage is that it exposes how hard you try to avoid pain in the way you love.

causes us to lose heart or harden our heart, and this cuts off the energetic flow between us. Yet if we can learn to make use of our pain, it can be an invaluable helper and guide on the path. For it exposes and directs our attention to places inside us where we are shut down, contracted, and half-asleep. If I can move with my pain more fluidly, my rigid defenses start to dissolve and I become more permeable to love's awakening influence."

I was not able to give myself vulnerably to Dawn until I saw that I'd approached love fearfully, trying to minimize the sacrifice and maximize the pleasure. As I began to see my defensiveness and the havoc it caused for both of us, I realized we needed to find a path through the disappointment into something larger.

However, even as I recognized all the ways our defensiveness was suffocating our marriage, I wasn't able to throw mine away. I certainly wasn't able to help Dawn throw hers away. This is where you need to call upon your Guide. Your vulnerability to disappointment will help you begin to pay attention to the Lord.

Paul wrote the Corinthians a scorching letter that, at first, he regretted sending. But when he saw how the pain from his words impacted them, he changed his mind. He wrote, "I am no longer sorry that I sent that letter to you, though I was sorry for a time, for I know that it was painful to you for a little while. Now I am glad I sent it, not because it hurt you, but because the pain caused you to have remorse and change your ways. It was the kind of sorrow God wants his people to have, so you were not harmed by us in any way," (2 Corinthians 7:8-9).

The pain in my marriage was something I could not run away from. I felt it inside and I saw it on Dawn's face. When it didn't stop, it exposed how "wretched and miserable and poor and blind and naked" (Revelation 3:17) I was. It brought me face-to-face with the Lord. I finally saw what I had avoided most of my life: I was not really on board with His "ministry of reconciliation." Dawn became the mirror I needed to help me see myself.

FORGIVENESS

If you are going to turn away from honoring your fleshly nature and the way it causes division and chaos in your marriage, you are going to have to recognize and accept your tendency to seek vengeance. Paul addresses the corrosive nature of acting out vengeance in relationships when he writes, "When others are happy, be happy with them. If they are sad, share their sorrow. Live in harmony with each other. Never pay back evil for evil to anyone. Dear friends, never avenge yourselves. Leave that to God," (Romans 12:15-17, 19).

This passage follows thirteen exhortations ranging from love of Christians to hospitality toward strangers. In each, we hear an expression of a heart that has tasted forgiveness and wants to live that out. Then the passage really slows down and changes mood, as if Paul lingers to tell his readers what to avoid. He writes, "Beloved, do all these things but don't do this: Don't avenge yourselves." He says vengeance stands in the way of living with forgiveness as a motivating dynamic in your relationships. Vengeance destroys relationships and redemptive love. He says, "Hate what is evil." Hate vengeance, for vengeance will pull you away from living with a forgiving heart.

Forgiveness comes as you let the Lord's love soften your disappointment so that you are more able to return kindness for an injury. In marriage it means being willing to move past a hurt or a wound so you can give yourself to your spouse for their good. Forgiveness means letting go of bitterness and resentment and reaching out for something better in a world that does not cooperate perfectly with your deepest longings. Forgiveness means agreeing with God's heart. It means you're willing to say, "I live in a fallen world, but I know I can trust God to work things together for good and I can participate with Him toward that end." It is being on board with what He wants to accomplish so much that you begin refusing the temptation to nurture your disappointment by holding others to the laws of perfection and performance. He loves you though you've hurt Him. Now you can do the same for others.

Oddly, marriage intensifies how much you experience disappointment and relational pain. You dreamed that marriage would forever erase those feelings from your life and when it didn't, you felt duped. But as the closeness of marriage helps you recognize that you can't achieve what you and your spouse want in your own strength, you have no other option than to turn to the mercy of God to begin feeling less alone and more beloved. *Remember, you don't turn to God because you have become a better person. You turn to Him because you face how unloving you and your spouse have been to each other.* You finally accept your need to receive love from Someone who naturally gives it to you unconditionally. The longer I stayed at marriage and let the pain of it draw me to the Lord, the more I began to move through the disappointment by letting Him care for me.

I can't tell you how long it took me to recognize and resist evil's lies. But slowly, and I mean very slowly, my commitment to the flesh began to be broken. In the midst of ongoing assault, I began to resist its pull and to ask God to have mercy on me for my foolishness. As I became more receptive to God's kindness, I started having more of it to share with Dawn. Christ in me was nurtured through the process of receiving forgiveness from God and sharing it with Dawn. Giving and receiving forgiveness becomes life-giving energy in a marriage of Common Ground.

REPENTANCE

Repentance is a change in direction. It involves not only resisting the way evil tries to pull you toward fleshly living, but actively forgiving your spouse by treating him or her with kindness. In Proverbs, the wise man warns, "Don't be impressed with your own wisdom. Instead, fear the Lord and turn your back on evil," (Proverbs 3:7). This is repentance.

As God softened me I was more able to slow down and listen to Dawn. This helped me to start choosing to do so as a way to love her, and that meant I was repenting of and confronting the pull of my flesh. In the deeply prideful years of my marriage, I was impatient and aggressive in our relationship. I wanted to get into and through the deep things without having the type of trust and friendship a solid relationship requires. I learned that real change is gradual and that I'd been too impatient to invest the time it takes to change – truly change – over the long haul. I had to submit to God and resist evil. Because the beliefs that supported my flesh were so entrenched in me, I experienced shame and condemnation when I tried to step out of them. This was evil trying to torment me back into self-reliance. Whenever I walked new pathways of resistance, evil tried to bully me away from them.

You probably have no idea how much faith and humility it takes to disarm evil in marriage – I didn't. I wanted steps or principles to take me around this battle with evil, instead of enduring through the shame and contempt evil heaped on us as we submitted to God's truth. Trusting my efforts and trying to get Dawn to fit into my way of doing things came naturally to me; it took me many years to soften so I could more readily say no to my flesh and yes to the Lord's ministry of reconciliation. David Powlison is so right when he writes, "Spiritual warfare with the power of evil is a matter of consistently and repeatedly turning from darkness to light in the midst of assailing darkness. Christians fight spiritual warfare by repentance, faith, and obedience."

Your attachment to the flesh is very strong. But you use God's mighty weapons (repentance and forgiveness) to knock down the devil's proud arguments that keep you and your spouse living in the flesh (2 Corinthians 10:3-5). The evil one may redouble his attack, but it won't be from a position of strength.

When Dawn and I painfully uncover ways we live in the flesh, agree on the fact that we hurt each other and move toward one another, we find that we pray more powerfully than at any other time in our relationship. "Then those who feared the Lord spoke with each other, and the Lord listened to what they said," (Malachi 3:16). *All the other things you do spiritually support the moments when you humbly admit sinning against and hurting your spouse (and you resist the pull to be defensive about it).* Those moments turn into prayers: "Lord, we are not good enough to earn a good marriage. Only You can give us that. We admit our need and ask You to help." You say that best through your honesty and humility.

You'll grow the faith to endure through the painful, humble moments when God helps you see the ways you live in the flesh. That's when you disarm the evil in your midst. I enjoy watching evil fall away in situations where Dawn or I have been bound. Redemption tastes very sweet – especially when I can share it with Dawn, the one I've hurt and suffered with the most.

REUNION

The great gift of our marriage is that it kept bringing Dawn and I to the end of ourselves. The more we experienced distance and division, the harder we tried to make marriage what we wanted it to be. Slowly, we recognized the foolishness in that, repented and began to be nurtured and cared for by the Lord in such a way that we were more energized to love like Him. Through long years we felt more loved by the Lord than we did by each other. In difficult periods we each kept turning to Him, crying out to him and asking Him to help. His kindness softened our vengeance. The way He comforted us and encouraged us began to help us taste what we really wanted and needed – a love that couldn't be earned or deserved. Over time we began to give more of that to each other, because we had tasted it from the Lord.

Jesus was able to endure the shame of the cross because of the joy His Father had set before Him (Hebrews 12:2). Common Ground comes on the other side of vengeance, blame, shame, division, and evil's terrible lies. I had to learn to pray like Jesus on the cross, "Father, forgive her. She doesn't know what she's doing," (Luke 23:34). At the same time, Dawn was learning to pray that prayer for me. We never thought that learning (and relearning) to let Jesus help us pray that prayer in marriage was going to be our path toward Common Ground, but it was. Here's the key, though – I first heard that prayer as Jesus prayed it for me. As I let Him care for me despite the fact that I kept resisting His call to love my wife and others, I learned how to extend that same kind of love to Dawn. It has made all the difference in the world.

Jesus loved me when I wasn't really able to love my wife. Through that great love, I began to grow a desire to love Dawn like Jesus loved me. Slowly I began to love Dawn better and she began to encourage me in truly meaningful ways. Somewhere on that steep, rocky mountain we'd chosen to climb together, we started listening to the Guide and taking His direction, and He brought us through our selfishness and our disappointment.

4
BURDENS

Because marriage unites a man with a woman, evil works to create confusion and drama around gender differences to sully what God ordains. Evil is a deceptive enemy, working to bully you away from togetherness. He will attempt to divide and conquer you, preying on your individual burdens as men and as women. Remember, he was there at Eden.

After Adam helped name the animals, it became clear that he was the only species without a mate. So God fashioned a companion who was suitable for him (Genesis 2:18-23). God then declared that this was good.

That was enough for Satan. If marriage was good in God's eyes, then evil decided to attack and desecrate the togetherness of all husbands and wives, forevermore.

After He created Adam and Eve, God told them, "Be fruitful and multiply and fill the earth and subdue it and have dominion over the fish of the sea and over the birds of the heavens and over every living thing that moves on the earth," (Genesis 1:28, ESV). When God gave the directive to "multiply and fill the earth," He was pointing humans toward procreation and social development. In essence, He was saying, "As people made in My image, you are intended to live in relationship. Go make that happen." He is telling Adam and Eve to start a family, which would eventually lead outward to extended families and clans or tribes.

When God directed Adam and Eve to "fill the earth and subdue it," he emphasized that humans are meaning-seeking creatures who desire to make a difference in their world. This can be as simple as clearing land for a dwelling or as sophisticated as leading a research team to a major medical breakthrough. In whatever form it takes, we were made to influence the world around us.

Men and women share desires in both spheres, but the Bible shows us that men were created to lean in the direction of impact (rule and subdue) while women were fashioned to move toward connection (be fruitful and multiply). This difference between men and women is affirmed as early as the creation account in Genesis, in the consequences that befell them when they sinned.

EVIL TWISTS THE NATURE OF THE BURDEN

God disciplined Adam by telling him he would have impact only as he learned to toil with the "thorns and thistles" of life, while he told Eve should would experience pain in bringing forth children and that she would want to control her husband without success, (Genesis 3:16-19). Adam would have to struggle to become a man of impact. Eve would endure through relational disappointment before she could become richly connected to those she loved. This has been true for every man and woman since.

God's burden became a training ground for all of us, as we now have to go through frustration to taste our deepest longings. This "training" provides humans the opportunity to grow a trusting, dependent and life-giving relationship with the Lord that will carry on into eternity. When God reordered the world by imposing these burdens, He was not resigning from the battle in frustration. He was upping the stakes by saying, "The chaos of evil will not thwart My plan. Now I will grow a deeper interdependent relationship between humans and Myself. These men and these women will have to learn to trust Me in the middle of difficulty, with no guarantee of getting what they want. They will have to learn radical, life-transforming trust."

> God finds hope, even in the sins of Adam and Eve and all of us who have followed them. Evil resents this.

So God finds hope, even in the sins of Adam and Eve and all of us who have followed them. Evil resents this, and has been trying ever since to twist this redemptive possibility into the reason husbands and wives give up on marriage.

What does that look like? When a man finds himself drowning, feeling like he is not making an impact in business or at home, it should point him to his need for God. Instead, evil likes for him to take it all personally, to become defensive, to resent his wife and rail against her. A wife follows her flesh and begrudges the relational disappointments that come with marriage. She resents her husband's inability to understand her disappointment, and instead she wants to manage it (and her husband), instead of allowing it to lead her to God. It's the burden turning them inside-out, and later on we'll explore in great depth the damage it can do in your marriage.

Marriage is often the one place it is hardest to run from God's redemptive discipline instituted through our respective burdens. As a husband lets the futility of marriage make him more pliable and lead him to God, he becomes a restored man. When a wife lets the relational disappointment of marriage draw her to God, she becomes a restored woman. As husbands and wives allow themselves to be softened and redeemed, God shows up all over and through them. Marriage, like few other entities in this world, demonstrates the hopeful, restorative nature of our burden. You can see why evil loves to use it to turn husbands and wives against each other instead, and how glad he is that our flesh so willingly conspires in the process.

ADAM & EVE WERE JUST LIKE US

Imagine the Garden of Eden before evil entered the picture. Adam and Eve are standing side by side in the midst of God's joy at His creation. Scripture records that "male and female He created them... they were both naked and were not ashamed... and God saw everything that He had made and behold, it was very good," (Genesis 1:27, 2:25, 1:31, ESV). *This is Common Ground in its purest form*, husband and wife standing together, vulnerable and unashamed in the midst of God's affirming presence.

Can you imagine how the enemy felt about that? A man and a woman, living freely and holy as God called them to, in His image? Evil is compelled to destroy the unique distinctions that allow God's creations to bring Him glory. Because we have a biblical account of how evil brought chaos to the first couple, it helps us to understand how evil works to sabotage Common Ground by attacking gender.

Dan Allender and Tremper Longman articulate it well in their book, *Intimate Allies*: "Let [us] remind you that we are made in the image of God as male and female. Somehow gender reflects something about God. A man reflects something about God's character that is different from a woman and vice versa... And God's enemy, Satan, wishes to destroy glory. The evil one cannot destroy God; therefore he tries to destroy the reflection of God: man and woman. His prime way of attempting to destroy glory is to make it too frightening to be truly a man or a woman and to offer counterfeit routes to live out gender." Evil initiated this attack on God's glory in the Garden of Eden. As you look closely at God's interaction with Adam and Eve (while Satan lurks in the background), you begin to understand how evil worked to bring chaos to the first marriage.

Let's back up and look a little closer at what took place in the Garden. After God created paradise, he told Adam to cultivate and protect it. To help Adam enjoy his new domain God gave him some additional guidance: "You may freely eat any fruit of every tree in the garden except fruit from the tree of the knowledge of good and evil," (Genesis 2:16-17). After this, God created Eve. There is no account of Adam relaying to Eve what God said about the forbidden fruit, but Adam must have told her. We know this because Satan starts his rebellion by lying to Eve about the consequences of eating from the tree. This lie pulls Eve into deception and she eats some of the forbidden fruit. However, evil's ploy to divide the first couple does not come to full fruition until Adam eats. That's when Common Ground is spoiled. Scripture says, "*At that moment* their eyes were opened, and they suddenly felt shame at their nakedness," (Genesis 3:7).

SATAN ATTACKS THE WIFE

Satan initiated his plan by starting with the wife. It is interesting to note that Satan only relates with Eve, but this is enough to pull both her and Adam away from God's command. Adam doesn't step into the conversation between Eve and Satan, and Eve doesn't turn to him after she is tempted.

In fact, when God curses Satan, He says, "From now on, you and the woman will be enemies," (Genesis 3:15). There is no direct mention of men in God's curse upon Satan. God focuses only on the relationship between women and Satan. He says that in the battle between good and evil, Satan will go after women as a way to advance his revolt.

The husband fails by not carrying out God's directives and by blaming this on his wife. After eating the forbidden fruit and experiencing shame for the first time, Adam and Eve covered themselves with fig leaves and went into hiding. God sought them out and asked Adam for a replay of the day's events. Adam failed to answer Him directly, instead blaming God (for creating Eve) and Eve (for eating first). By failing to take any responsibility, Adam's denial moves him farther away from both God and his wife.

Recall, God doesn't agree with Adam's assessment of the situation. Even though Eve ate first, the New Testament gives a simple but profound summary of Adam's role by noting that "Adam sinned," (Romans 5:12). It's similar to what I see played out each day in my work as a counselor. Adam, the first husband, failed to get involved as Satan was tempting his wife. Had Adam simply clung to what God had told him, it would have propelled him to intervene on Eve's behalf against Satan. It would have strengthened both of them against evil's temptation to defy God's direction.

The wife was deceived as Satan spun a little truth into a much bigger lie. Satan slithered his way into the middle of Common Ground with lies that were based in truth. He threw Eve a curveball by suggesting that God didn't have her best interests at heart. He said, "Did God really say you must not eat any of the fruit in the garden?" (Genesis 3:1).

Satan recounted the basic storyline, but suggested that God said they couldn't eat from *any of the trees*, instead of just the one. He cast God's caring words into a misleading story by suggesting that God was holding out on them. Eve responded, clarifying that she and Adam had God's permission to eat from all the trees except one. As she talked with Satan she repeated God's words but added a little twist of her own. She said they couldn't eat from the tree or *touch it*. Eve was pulled into Satan's game of adding to God's words. Immediately, Satan's tone changes and he seems to become excited. Noticing that Eve "improved" on what God had ordained, Satan suggested that instead of dying, Eve would actually become wiser if she ate from the tree. His inference? That by taking the matter into her own hands she could end up in a better place than where she'd started. She was convinced and she tasted of the forbidden fruit.

Imagine if Adam and Eve had stood *together* to battle evil.

We can't be sure exactly how Eve's behavior impacted Adam. We know only that she influenced the result. Somehow, being pulled into evil's deception contributed to their failure as a couple. The New Testament records, "And it was the woman, not Adam, who was deceived by Satan, and sin was the result," (1 Timothy 2:14). Eve contributed to evil's plot by listening to him and agreeing with his accusation that God was holding out on them. From there, all she could do was watch as evil's plan gave birth to the sin that Adam finalized when he ate.

When it comes to marital harmony – or remaining on Common Ground that evil wants to disrupt – you have to submit to God and resist evil as a couple and he will flee (James 4:7). Consider what might have happened if Adam had stepped into the conversation between Eve and Satan. Perhaps together they would have held onto

God's truth. Did watching his wife fall into deception deflate Adam? Did his initial lack of courage make it easier to abandon God's words when he held the fruit of the tree in his hands? Imagine if Eve had turned and looked at her husband after Satan tempted her. Would acknowledging her husband have helped them remember God's words? What if she had asked, "Adam, what was it God said about that forbidden fruit?" Might that have brought them together against evil?

We will never know exactly what could have happened but we do know that Adam and Eve did not battle evil together. Once evil entered the picture, they acted independently of one another and turned away from God's advice. God's words didn't matter enough to Adam, so he failed to have the courage to step between his wife and evil. He failed to tend and protect what God had given him. A husband fights evil best by stepping between his wife and the ways evil tries to tempt her. Eve needed to challenge the temptation to take matters into her own hands. She should have opposed evil by turning to her husband, or by waiting for him. A wife fights evil best by resisting and waiting.

MODERN-DAY ADAM AND MODERN-DAY EVE

I see very few couples that fight together against evil this way. Instead, I regularly run into couples that are separated from each other because of the work of evil. It is eerie how many couples come through my door struggling in exactly the same way. Regularly, I meet an uninvolved husband who does not recognize how much his wife is struggling with the way evil lies to her. When I ask him to get involved with what's going on with his wife, he gets a deer-in-the-headlights expression. He's convinced that his wife is far too difficult to deal with, and that is why he has stopped relating to her. Because he is not visibly upset, he doesn't realize how subtly condescending he is in the way he talks about her. In fact, he often implies that they're in my office so I can *fix* her. Such a husband is typically unaware that he has abandoned his wife's heart, which God asked him to tend and protect.

On the other hand, the wife is normally more upset and despairing. She can readily recount all the problems in their marriage. What often strikes me is not all the detail she uses in describing the marital problems, but her enjoyment in describing them. Her passion and connection to their problems make her words sharper because of all the energy involved in her description. Because she has listened to evil's suggestion that God is holding out on her, she struggles with the state of their marriage more intensely than the husband. Examples of her husband's failures and passivity become huge neon signs flashing in her mind, and this weights her down even more. She is often tired and frustrated of dealing with evil, but isn't going to resist him and certainly will not wait for her husband.

Consider what happened in the Garden of Eden as an example of how evil attacks you as individuals. A wife gets worn out by Satan's lies and thinks less of her husband. Her husband justifies his passivity and blames her for their problems. Evil continues to incite marital division by tempting and trying the wife.

This is not what God intended or what He desires for either of you. A husband can learn to genuinely care for his wife and sacrificially involve himself with her. A wife can learn to appreciate her husband and cooperate with his love. God gives us powerful gifts so that we can come together against evil. As a husband and wife understand their unique gifts and God's purpose behind them, they can join together with God in the battle against evil.

HIS GIFTS, HER GIFTS

Joining together with your spouse and following God toward Common Ground begins with recognizing your gifts. Evil desperately wants to divide you and spoil the togetherness you can experience. You already know how stealthily he exploits the unique differences between you and your spouse. He does this because he wants to defile God and the gifts He has given you. However, as you understand how God has created you, either as a man or as a woman, you begin the walk toward Common Ground.

A husband is equipped in two areas, which I'll call the outer gift (physical strength) and the inner gift (relational resilience), which are unique to men. That's not to say there are not strong women; we know there are. And it's not to say we haven't ever witnessed women who move through relational breakdowns with ease. But men have been endowed with gifts that, when used unselfishly in marriage, can help their wives feel more at rest and more connected.

For much of the rest of the book, I'm going to articulate my understanding of the ways God would have us mesh together as husbands and wives, both spiritually and emotionally. Still, you might find you and your spouse might not fit the molds. There was a time I would have argued we didn't, either.

For instance, more than twenty years ago when I first heard that men tend to be passive toward relationship, I would have insisted that didn't square with my experience. I was sure I was far more active in trying to talk about things and communicate than my wife. Over the seasons of our marriage, not only have I changed, but my perspective has changed as well. What I initially thought was a passion to connect with my wife was really a fearful and selfish preoccupation to get my needs met by insisting we hash over every nuance of every disagreement, whether Dawn wanted to or not. As I have become more unselfish, Dawn's relational desires have surfaced and mine reflect more masculine tendencies. If, while reading, you find that you or your spouse fall outside the common gender differences I describe, let those instances create questions for reflection and discovery.

THE MAN'S OUTER GIFT

God gave men bigger frames and stronger muscles than women. Peter was thinking of this when he wrote, "You husbands must give honor to your wives. Treat her with understanding as you live together. She may be weaker than you are, but she is your equal partner in God's gift of new life. If you don't treat her as you should, your prayers will not be heard," (1 Peter 3:7).

The readers in Peter's audience were living in a culture where men often subjugated women, who had almost no defenses. Peter was saying to the husbands, "In a culture blind to the ways of God, preach the Gospel to your wife by resisting the temptation to use your physical advantages to suppress her. Instead use them to serve her and care for her."

The meaning of "weaker vessel" in this passage is strictly physical. Men have always been, on average, taller and stronger. This physical difference is a gift God gives a husband to use in the service of others. Biblical teaching makes clear that God gives gifts to people so that they can be a blessing to others (Genesis 12:2-3). Unfortunately, men often use the physical gift brutishly and women become the victims. Throughout time, women have been raped, beaten, and robbed because they were not physically strong enough to defend themselves or to escape.

As a result, women can find themselves feeling uneasy in the presence of men – even when they're in no danger of being harmed. Most men don't realize how frequently women are affected in this way, in general and especially in their close relationships. The physical discrepancy in marriage can create daily apprehension in a wife unless the quality of the marital relationship is sound enough to neutralize her fear. A husband and wife can have the same level of maturity, and even the same humility and self-control. But in day-to-day living, the wife legitimately feels more physical danger than her husband, because he is bigger and stronger. This can change the way she relates to her husband on a regular basis. When a man becomes aware and understands this difference, he can be more considerate as a way to disarm it.

A simple example: One of the biggest complaints I hear from wives is that their husbands fail to help carry the load around the house. Note that I used the word "carry." Maintaining a household is backbreaking work, and a husband can serve his wife physically by carrying a large part of the burden with day-to-day chores. Oftentimes, however, a man uses his physical advantage selfishly. He shouts, bullies, threatens, or even strikes his wife. He also might sit on the couch and expect the wife to carry more of the physical burden around the house. Every one of those examples shows a man using his outer gift *against* his wife, not *for* her.

THE MAN'S INNER GIFT

At the very core of their beings, a man and a woman are different in what they want out of life. They approach marriage out of this difference and it can bring the same type of tension as the physical differences.

Earlier, we noted that God burdened Adam with futility to frustrate his desire to have impact. At the same time, He burdened Eve with disappointment in relationships to frustrate her desire to be connected. They were both burdened in the area of their deepest desires.

Hear this: The burden in Genesis makes clear that the marriage relationship will be more vexing for the wife. A wife's burden is specifically worked out in the marital relationship in a way that her husband's is not. A wife will experience more intense frustration in relationship (Genesis 3:16) that her husband will escape. This is the crux of the inner gift: The marital relationship is easier for the husband than it is for the wife. Not easy, but *easier*. Marriage is more tenuous for a wife because she longs for more in marriage than her husband does, and she is wounded more

> The burden in Genesis makes clear that the marriage relationship will be more vexing for the wife than it is for her husband.

67

deeply by marital pain. When you really want something, it's more crushing when you don't get it.

Therefore, a husband has more relational resilience. The disappointments in marriage are not as debilitating. God endowed a husband with this resilience so that he could keep turning toward the wife trying to bring the couple together while he aims to be thoughtful and considerate. When a husband uses his gift unselfishly in this way and keeps sacrificing for his wife, she will feel safe and cared for. This helps a wife trust in her husband, and in his love for her.

THE WIFE'S GIFTS: BEAUTY, RELATIONAL WISDOM, SPIRITUAL SENSITIVITY

By the very way she is created and lives her life, a wife can inspire her husband toward reconciliation with God so he is empowered to tend and protect the territory the Lord entrusts to him. After God created Adam, He said, "It is not good that the man should be alone; I will make him a helper fit for him," (Genesis 2:18, ESV). At the sight of Eve, Adam declared, "At last! She is part of my own flesh and bone!" (Genesis 2:23).

Adam was stirred when he first saw Eve. He was inspired and motivated. What was it about her that moved him? Her physical beauty was arousing, but that alone was not what moved Adam. In fact, Scripture warns against the danger of being attracted solely to physical beauty. "Don't lust for her beauty. Don't let her coyness seduce you," (Proverbs 6:25). In that Proverb, the adulterous woman was physically alluring but dangerous, because union with her advanced unfaithfulness.

God's beauty affirmed in Scripture is the exact opposite. His beauty is based in His selfless but celebratory faithfulness. God's nature is love (1 John 4:8) because He exists as three unique beings who relate so well they are called one God. Human nature is naturally selfish, so you don't readily grasp the heights and depths of God's beauty that are reflected in his ability to love unselfishly. When the Psalmist wrote, "Honor and majesty surround Him; strength and beauty are in His sanctuary," (Psalm 96:6) one quality he was celebrating was the exquisite beauty of supportive, unselfish love. Pause and consider how different you feel when you are in a relationship with someone who gets you, and supports you and sacrifices for you. This is how the trinity relates all the time.

When the Scriptures address a woman's beauty, it points to her potential to reflect God's beauty and promote faithfulness to Him and His kind of loyal love. Human beings are hard-wired to worship. Winston Smith writes, "Worship is not simply the intentional act of bowing down before a chosen deity. Rather, worship describes man's inescapable need to organize his life around the pursuit of something greater than himself." A wife's beauty is specifically designed to help a husband pursue a beauty larger then her, which assists him in deepening his worship of God. The most exquisite taste of beauty a human can experience comes with entering into the never-ending, loyal love of the trinity. Adam was stirred when he saw Eve because there was something about her that called him to join together with God.

The fact that we are all worshippers and that a woman reflects God's beauty means that a wife can use her beauty to coerce a man to revolve around *her*. Or she can make it about their need – as a couple – to join with God. In *The Weight of Glory*, C.S. Lewis writes, "We do not want merely to see beauty, though, God knows, even that is bounty enough. We want something else which can hardly be put into words – to be united with the beauty we see, to pass into it, to receive it into ourselves, to bathe in it, to become part of it." Lewis knew our desire to get lost in beauty was connected to our desire to be reconciled to God. But the power of a woman's beauty means she also can be tempted to exploit it. "Charm is deceptive and beauty does not last, but a woman who fears the Lord will be greatly praised," (Proverbs 31:30). When a wife's deep trust lies in the Lord, she doesn't mix her charm and physical beauty together to make things about her. She lets her inner beauty be a reflection of the Lord's loyal love.

Beauty exposes your humanness or brokenness because it brings you in contact with God's glory and holiness. It moves you outside of yourself. Every husband has a choice. Either he can feel that he doesn't measure up, or he can reach for more – from God. It is like what happened when Isaiah saw the Lord sitting on his throne, "high and lifted up," (Isaiah 6:1, ESV). Coming in contact with ultimate beauty evoked this response from Isaiah: "My destruction is sealed, for I am a sinful man and a member of sinful race," (Isaiah 6:5).

> When a wife's beauty is mixed with kindness, she becomes a compelling force in her husband's life.

After Isaiah is reduced to humble contrition at the sight of God's beauty, a seraph touches his lips with a coal and says, "Now your guilt is removed, and your sins are forgiven," (Isaiah 6:7). Next, we find Isaiah willingly responding to the Lord's request to go and preach to His people. Beauty and kindness together inspired courage in Isaiah. He was moved to stand up and follow the Lord. When a wife's beauty is mixed with kindness, she becomes a compelling force in her husband's life. That is why wives are encouraged to make themselves attractive by the good things they do (1 Timothy 2:10) or to clothe themselves with the beauty that comes from within the unfading beauty of a gentle and quiet spirit (1 Peter 3:4). Cultivating inner feminine beauty powerfully inspires a man toward good. In fact, the Apostle Peter encouraged wives that their inner beauty had the power to win over unbelieving husbands (1 Peter 3:1-2).

In addition to beauty, a wife often has the relational and spiritual sensitivity that are required to inspire her husband toward more. A husband often doesn't engage with his wife in order to satisfy his longing for impact, because he finds less complicated ways to secure this outside the marriage. This often leaves a wife with an underlying sense of vulnerability. Scripture teaches that those who are more vulnerable in this world are predisposed to recognize Kingdom values, because they regularly experience the opposite. For example, a child who has grown up in a home with domestic violence experiences cruelty and therefore hungers and thirsts for a home of safety. When you experience injustice, it helps you to see and cry out for justice. It enables you to see how things *could* be. "Christians who are poor should be glad, for God has honored them. Listen to me, dear brothers and sisters. Hasn't God chosen the poor in this world to be rich in faith?" (James 1:9, 2:5).

In the context of marriage, a wife's relational vulnerability often gives her clear vision to know what life-giving relationship could look like. A husband's gifts, if harbored selfishly, will turn him toward relational passivity and indifference. Because fidelity to relationship is so central to the nature of Christian maturity, a man's indifference to relationship often fosters spiritual blindness. A woman's vulnerability in this world does the opposite – it gives her spiritual sensitivity. The women Jesus knew were more attentive to Him in his hour of need, and they anticipated His resurrection more noticeably than the men.

This relational wisdom and spiritual sight is an additional gift a wife is given to assist her in helping her husband. She recognizes clearly where her husband is not devoted in his relationships with God or others. She can distinctly visualize his relational and spiritual possibilities more acutely than he does. She is uniquely qualified to encourage him into more. This gift can be misused to disparage a husband, if a wife constantly points out what he ought to be doing. However, when given in love, this gift helps a wife empower her husband to make connections with God and with what God desires, so he can go after it with passion. A wife's gift of relational wisdom and spiritual sensitivity can be used to propel a man toward deeper faithfulness.

Together, a husband and wife are uniquely designed to fight evil well. When a husband uses his physical strength and relational resilience to care for and protect his wife against evil, her trials and temptations will not have the same impact. Her beauty, relational wisdom and spiritual sensitivity will all become more vibrant and help the husband stay passionately faithful to the Lord. When a wife resists the lies of evil and uses her gifts to encourage the husband toward the Lord, his passion to cooperate with the Lord and stand against evil is emboldened. He will remember and stand for the things the Lord has told him. When a husband and wife use their gifts to bless each other, Common Ground is not far away.

PART II

The rest of this book describes how God calls you to cooperate with Him and follow pathways that will help you move, more and more, into Common Ground.

This is the practical part of the book. When it comes to hands-on marital advice, most couples want specific, "do-able" tasks that will ensure them a happier marriage. But when it came to addressing issues like togetherness, Jesus and the New Testament writers frequently pointed others to internal change, not to explicit outward behavior. This often involved wise counsel to turn away from misguided beliefs and actions in order to surrender to a more life-giving way of participating with God. Jesus said it this way: "Whoever clings to his life will lose it, and whoever loses this life will save it," (Luke 17:33).

The section begins with a synthesis of God's scriptural counsel to the husband (Base Camp: The Husband's Calling) and follows with the three primary ways he can follow that call. Then, similarly, we outline the wife's biblical calling, and the ways she can follow it as she relates to her husband.

The pages ahead will present ways of relating with your spouse and the Lord that will bring real life to your marriage. There is a more life-giving marriage ahead for you, and these pathways can help you find your way there.

BASE CAMP: A HUSBAND'S CALLING

At this point I ask you to accept that men and women are created differently for a holy purpose – God's design. But in the world, the evil one attempts to exploit the differences. *The first part of a husband's calling is to recognize that he has been given gifts that leave him with something to do for and give to his wife.*

For years I subtly mocked that marriage was hard for Dawn. Many of the things I said carried this inference: "If you were as mature as I am, you wouldn't be suffering so much." I had no idea her struggles were different than mine because evil was pursuing her in a way he was not pursuing me. Because of my own fear and selfishness, I resisted God's call to give myself more sacrificially for my wife. I'm ashamed to say that instead, I unknowingly belittled her struggle.

When the Holy Spirit illuminated the truth to me, I was humbled – it was a beautiful humility. It was my first move toward genuinely becoming a husband. The Scriptures are clear – men have been created with certain gifts – and I finally recognized what had always been true. I no longer felt justified in my passive indifference to my wife's heartache as a woman. Not only that, but I was beginning to understand that marriage is something much greater, much bigger than I'd ever imagined.

Husbands, as you begin the journey into Common Ground, it is important to understand that the biblical counsel God provides for you is different than what He gives to your wives. Remember, from those first days in Eden He's set men apart as beings who will labor to make an impact, and His guidance is designed to help you work through and overcome those struggles.

Evil works to mask and sabotage the beauty of God's presence. For example, you're called to love your wife, so evil wants you to be blinded to what biblical love really looks like. Evil will do whatever it takes to confuse you and trip you up. If you take the time to grasp your calling as a husband and remember that God will support you in that call, you will better recognize evil's attacks and be freer to walk toward redemption in your marriage.

MARRIAGE AS A CALLING

Because we're guys, the easiest thing for us to do is to call marriage a job. We identify with this. We get it. We can wrap our brains around what's expected of us. Problem is, that doesn't even begin to describe marriage as the calling that it is – an avenue to grow your faith and learn to rely more and more upon the Lord.

Only as your marriage helps you identify with the Lord will you grow the strength to love your wife well. This means you acknowledge that you're married to someone who needs your prayers and your understanding, even when she's hurt you – and often, at the very moment she's hurting you. *Remember, Christ has forgiven you more times than your spouse will ever need to.* To grow a marriage of Common Ground, it helps to recognize that marriage provides you with an opportunity to share in Christ's sufferings and in His ministry of reconciliation. As you acknowledge that God is calling you to marriage as a way to grow the character of Christ, you will be better prepared to endure through the ongoing difficulty that every husband and wife will face.

In addition, viewing marriage as a calling from God helps you to remember that you need His help to fulfill your calling. That help comes largely from following his messages to you in the Scriptures and relying upon the support He wants to give you along the way. The Bible is a revelation of God's heart. Biblical commands provide not only direction on how to aim your life, but as often as you turn to it, you're reminded again of your need for the Lord's help.

My calling as a husband has been a conduit for me to need, wrestle with, cry out to, and lean on God all the years I have been married. He has used it to shape and enlarge my faith in too many ways to count. As you view marriage as something bigger than a role or task, you will more naturally look to God and to His Word.

SACRIFICE FOR YOUR WIFE

Husbands, God commands us to live sacrificially for our wives, to give up our own comfort for them as Christ did for the Church. Eugene Peterson does a masterful job paraphrasing this passage in Ephesians in *The Message*: "Husbands, go all out in your love for your wives, exactly as Christ did for the Church – a love marked by giving, not getting. Christ's love makes the Church whole. His words evoke her beauty. Everything he does and says is designed to bring the best out of her, dressing her in dazzling white silk, radiant with holiness. And that is how husbands ought to love their wives," (Ephesians 5: 25-28).

This deliberate move toward your wife for her good helps her become more beautiful in the same way Christ's sacrifice made the Church holy and clean. As you embody Christ by unselfishly caring for your wife, evil has less freedom to harass her. Your sacrifice helps disarm evil's lies and thus helps enrich your wife's faith so she becomes more beautiful on the inside. This makes her more striking, because a wife's genuine loveliness comes "from within, the unfading beauty of a gentle and quiet spirit," (1 Peter 3:4).

Be warned. When the book of Ephesians comes up in conversation about marriage, many people skip over the part about sacrifice and giving. Instead, they like to talk about the wife's submission and the husband's headship. Don't fall into this trap. Biblical headship actually has more to do with serving and reconciling than with decision-making or power. The Greek word for "head" in Paul's writing means "to bring together." The head brings together the alienated parts just as Jesus healed the rift between man and God. Through a husband's sacrifice, he helps to disarm the tension between himself and his wife, allowing them to draw closer together.

SHOW UNDERSTANDING

Another major New Testament command directs you to display understanding toward your wife. Peter calls husbands to "give honor to your wives. Treat her with understanding as you live together. She may be weaker than you are, but she is your equal partner in God's gift of new life," (1 Peter 3:7). The King James version says it another way: "Dwell with them according to knowledge."

That translation helps answer the question, "Why is there so much tension in male and female relationships?" It's because husbands have so little knowledge of their wives. In Greek, the word "dwell" means to reside together, but the word for "knowledge" implies that an inquiry has taken place and new information has been realized. Putting the words together, I want to suggest the husband is to bring the couple together by being interested in and getting to know his wife, not by "fixing her" or taking any other action to make her seem less burdensome to him. Peter is telling you to fight through the times you are afraid, annoyed or angered by your wife's angst. Instead, let every situation become an opportunity to get to know your wife better and to relate to her with more understanding.

When you use your gifts to become more curious about your wife, you foster harmony. Basically, what Peter says is this: "In a world where people regularly use their advantages to exploit others, as a husband you are to be radically different. Instead of using your gifts for yourself, they are there to help you be patient with your wife and interested in what interests her. This disarms the fleshly tension evil intensifies and helps your wife feel safer and more at home with you. If, however, you use your gifts selfishly to turn away from your wife or to bully her, the tension between the two of you will thicken."

> The husband is to bring the couple together by being interested in his wife, not by "fixing her" or trying to make her seem less burdensome to him.

When you aim to grow understanding, you help create an atmosphere in which your wife feels wanted and at rest. As you fight your flesh to become more interested in your wife, your actions say to her, "Who you are matters. I'm not here to control you or to use you. I am here to follow the Lord and I care about you." As you do that, evil is disarmed.

WHAT IT LOOKS LIKE

I remember the first time I consciously tried to embody this concept in my own marriage. It was toward the end of a three-day weekend, and it had become painfully obvious to me that I'd been hard to live with. What was also clear was that Dawn was having an even harder time being honest with me about it.

So I said to her, "Honey, I know I've been rough on you this weekend. I know it hasn't been easy. I want you to explain to me what is has been like for you to live with me and I am not going to answer you back. I will think on it at least for three days before I say anything."

Her response showed that my posture helped her have some courage in this situation. Here's what was on her heart, and I'd never heard it before: "You know how you go to the summer carnival every year but never win a stuffed animal? You're all excited about the carnival coming to town and you dream of finally winning something. You shoot the water in the clown's mouth and throw the softballs at the milk bottles but nothing ever works. Well, imagine the summer you finally win that stuffed animal – that is what it would feel like to me if we could laugh in this house."

I wept in response to Dawn's words for two reasons. I was able to invite her toward me with strength and she responded. But I also wept because what Dawn said was true, and the Holy Spirit gave me the spiritual eyes I needed to see it and let it pierce me to the core. So I was weeping tears of repentance as well as tears of joy. I had become more humble, but I had witnessed Dawn growing in strength.

Jesus gave Dawn what she needed to speak truth to me. Most of her life, Dawn had avoided difficult situations, preferring to withdraw or make jokes instead of trying to speak words of truth.

Although it felt foreign and risky to her, it was an act of great faith and love that allowed our marriage to move in a new direction.

In the past, there were times when I'd bullied Dawn. I'd pick a fight, or refuse to leave her alone until I was convinced she understood *my* point of view. This time, however, I laid down my gift of strength beforehand and offered her justice by letting her know it was safe to be honest. And instead of running away from conflict, Dawn responded with courage and truth, which helped to facilitate redemption. At the moment she was wounding me profoundly, she seemed more beautiful than ever.

WHAT GETS IN THE WAY

Men, it's possible you now have a clearer grasp on your calling and the gifts you've been given to help you respond to it. That understanding is huge. Understand, too, that the world and your own human nature are going to interfere as you try to use those gifts. I've seen four ways this happens to most guys:

- Relationship carelessness
- Futility
- Selfishness
- Spiritual interference

Relationship carelessness: Because I live with four women, somebody's always talking about relationships. Every once in a while, my daughters will talk about whose volleyball team won that day in gym class, but it never dominates their conversations. They focus more on their friends, their friends' friends, their friends' boyfriends, and who's dating whom. They work at and worry about the quality of their relationships. So, because they pay attention to and analyze relationships a lot more than guys their age, I can see they are gaining more experience about how relationships work. Typically, girls have more interest in and access to jobs like babysitting, where they get to practice the responsibility of caring for other human beings. So it's no surprise that women are generally more prepared on the relationship front than men when they get to marriage – they've been working at it for years.

It seems ironic that a husband is called to care deeply for his wife when that's really her specialty, but it's true. This is the first major obstacle a husband encounters when he attempts to follow his call from God. Essentially in marriage, a husband steps up to bat as a Little Leaguer under the scrutiny of a wife, the Hall of Fame relationship coach who wants to win the championship.

> Husbands, you have to dig deep to find the courage to care for your wives, because it will mean you'll start facing a more direct spiritual attack.

Futility: If it isn't enough that God calls a man to love and care for a woman who is more attuned to his calling than he is, the difficulty intensifies when you include his burden in the obstacles he encounters. Remember, God has already disciplined men with futility, so we have to look to Him for help. Here's the daunting bottom line: Encountering daily futility means a husband will never care for his wife with any regular success. He will experience a measure of ineffectiveness his whole married life and yet he is called to stay at it with endurance. So, as a husband learns to sacrifice in caring for his wife, not only does he step up to bat with a competitive coach, but he's guaranteed to strike out. Often.

Selfishness: A husband is called to consider his wife's needs as more important than his own. Now, if you accept the fact that we have an inborn selfishness we must learn to fight, then you are in touch with how hard that will be.

It takes great faith for a husband to stand up to the reality of relationship carelessness, futility, and selfishness all at the same time. So to continue marking up the scorebook, you're being evaluated by a professional coach, you'll strike out far more than you connect, and your selfishness means you'll have a natural propensity to swing wildly, so much so that it will take great practice and focus to develop a smooth, even swing to have any chance at making contact at all. (It's helpful to keep in mind that baseball's all-time great hitters – Ted Williams, Hank Aaron, Cal Ripken, Jr. – only hit the ball about a third of the time.) A quality husband, because of all the obstacles he faces, only sacrifices and cares well a small amount of time. But he keeps swinging with passion.

Amazingly, there's more – **spiritual attack**. Remember, evil seeks out the vulnerable and more regularly attacks a wife to get at the marriage. Few men realize that their fear in engaging their wives is really their own fear of evil. They are afraid to step in between their wives and evil because once they do, evil will begin harassing them. It's easier not to get involved. Husbands, you have to dig deep to find the courage to care for your wives, because it will mean you'll have to start facing a more direct spiritual attack.

I cannot tell you how many times I have gotten angry at Dawn or at myself for an interference that was mostly energized by the evil one. I was extremely unprepared to deal with the amount of spiritual warfare I would encounter once I moved toward my wife and tried to care for her when she was in difficulty. Not to make light of it by bringing the baseball image home, but spiritual interference is like standing in the batter's box facing a 98-mph fastball while somebody pokes you in the side with a sharp stick.

STEADFAST LOVE

With all that husbands encounter in caring for their wives, it's really not much of a surprise that many men just drop their bats and head for the dugout. In our culture, know-how and performance are glorified. It's assumed that a man should be doing well – or know why he isn't, and be working hard to fix it. Our culture doesn't value the richer and more meaningful aspects of faith, such as prayerfully waiting, enduring, or humbling yourself under the mighty hand of God as He slowly works to help you.

To accurately comprehend your calling, you have to grab hold of your need for endurance and comprehend how much more important that is than know-how or performance. *Getting it right will never be as important as the quality of your faith and your heart.* The Lord doesn't see things the way you see them. People judge by outward appearance, but the Lord looks at the heart (1 Samuel 16:7).

No matter how accomplished or able a man is, he cannot become a good husband without more failure than he ever dreamed possible. In the midst of this failure, he will have to hold onto a belief that God can use it to grow his heart. A husband must battle the tendency to think he is supposed to get it right and instead keep aiming to be sacrificial and understanding, while feeding on God's grace in the midst of failure. As he feeds on God's redemptive love, it will transform him. He will have more freedom to endure with his wife. He will grow a steadfast heart. By hanging onto the Lord through repeated difficulty, a husband will learn with Paul that God's grace is sufficient for him and he will become content with "weaknesses and with insults, hardships, persecutions, and calamities," (2 Corinthians 12:8-10) because it will grow Christ's character in him.

"What is desired in a man is steadfast love," (Proverbs 19:22, ESV), not perfect performance. Biblically, a husband who demonstrates enduring love moves a wife most. Such a husband is defined by his willingness to keep trying to bring the couple together despite failure.

The book of Proverbs was written to young men to teach them how to grow into wiser older men, so it includes a great deal of wisdom on the themes that are important to men and their maturity. One such theme is diligence. Consider these two verses: "The soul of the sluggard craves and gets nothing, while the soul of the diligent is richly supplied," (Proverbs 13:4, ESV) and "the plans of the diligent lead surely to abundance, but everyone who is hasty comes only to poverty," (Proverbs 21:5, ESV). In the light of all the futility a man faces, he will be overwhelmed, so it makes sense that diligence is a key emphasis in developing genuine masculinity.

Diligence or steadfastness means to stay at something. It does not mean working like crazy or haphazardly throwing a lot of energy at a task. It means passionately remaining involved in the process. When I was first married, I wouldn't have been comforted by the thought that I needed to just keep *trying* to be sacrificial and understanding, trusting that over time God would honor my efforts and grow my heart to become more steadfast in the way Christ loved His Church. I had no category to believe that in the midst of chaos, confusion, and failure, Christ would come alive in me, strengthen my heart, and help me look beyond my failures. But that is exactly what happened. If you are going to learn to use your gifts to become genuinely sacrificial and understanding toward your wife, you will have to grow in steadfastness. Genuine biblical steadfastness mocks the complexity you face because it says, "I only have to do my part and God will do the rest."

Steadfastness is a gift to any wife. *As a man grows deeper character – as he is able to stay patiently at the task in front of him despite the complexity and failure it involves – his wife begins to experience rest.* She begins to see that her man is still alive to her despite all the difficulty he has encountered. She feels more invited to open up and give herself to him. A wife in the presence of a husband with steadfast love will come alive.

DEFIANT HUMILITY

I once wrote a newsletter called *Every Husband Feels Like a Jerk and Every Wife Agrees*. For guys, that feeling seems to evolve from a sense that they haven't and never will please their wives, and that their wives beat them up because of it. You know what happens next, maybe because you've lived it: Husband withdraws, becomes totally exasperated with wife, or feels completely defeated because no matter what he does, it's never good enough to meet her standards. This became such a common theme with the couples I saw that I knew we needed to find a way past this stumbling block so they could continue together toward Common Ground.

Here's what I found interesting, though: Most of the men I worked with *were* trying to love their wives the way they believed God called them to. They didn't begin by feeling indifferent; they ended there.

God calls a husband to love his wife sacrificially and to treat his wife with understanding over the long haul. So often a husband turns it into a job, an activity, making the discussion about what he *does* for his wife – working to provide for her, fixing things around the house, helping with the children. When this type of sacrifice doesn't reach into a wife's heart and satisfy her, she begins to make her disappointment known, either passively (by withdrawing) or actively (with unkind words). This pushes a husband to try harder or to withdraw. When neither of those strategies succeeds, a husband will often begin to feel a subtle anger at himself or at his wife. His efforts are not being affirmed. Yes, you're trying to show her love, doing the things that come naturally to you and that feel comfortable to you. But along the way the evil one will be telling your wife that you should be doing better.

Don't mix up taking out the garbage with the kind of relationship sacrifices that God really calls you to make in marriage. God (and every wife) wants a husband to love from a much deeper place. David articulates this perfectly in the Psalms when he says, "You would not be pleased with sacrifices, or I would bring them... The sacrifice you want is a broken spirit. A broken and repentant heart, O God, you will not despise," (Psalm 51:16-17). God wants your hearts to soften in marriage so that you love out of your depths. But a man often starts by trying to find the easiest path to make his spouse happy without his heart being softened.

Almost every husband starts out in marriage trying dutifully to please his wife. Few wives are prepared to respond to this with a healthy mixture of grace and truth. Thus, most couples get caught up in focusing on the husband's *performance*. This is because neither husband nor wife wants to really embrace the difficult journey of marriage, so the husband doesn't offer much and the wife often keeps trying to get him to change.

This misguided focus is exactly what evil wants. He tries to make the husband's performance the defining aspect of marital satisfaction.

Evil wants to pull husbands into feeling like they can't or don't care about their wives. Evil wants wives to be standing in judgment over their husbands, saturated with disappointment. Evil wants what the husband does (or doesn't do) or what he says (or doesn't say) to be the focus of the marriage. Meanwhile, evil wants to establish the wife's assessment of the husband's performance as the barometer on how the couple is doing.

Once both husband and wife are entrenched in watching the husband's performance, it becomes easier for evil to cast the husband's mistakes into the lie that he never cared about his wife and never really will. Why does this trick work so effectively? It's because a husband will never perform with regular success. His *heart* is much more important than his performance, but a couple has to grow and mature before a man's heart becomes what defines him. Along the way, they have to get out of the trap of focusing on what the husband does and shift toward caring about how they both love.

DEFIANT HUMILITY IN PRACTICE

Husbands, I'm going to outline the process of defiant humility and how I've seen it work to begin to change a man's heart, to redirect the couple's focus, and to rescue their marriage. Remember, it's evil you need to defy, not God and not your wife.

Abandon defensiveness: The first step is to grow the courage to admit that you fail to perform well enough to satisfy your wife on a regular basis. In marriage, evil always magnifies the husband's outward failures and makes them seem bigger. He continually assaults the wife, trying to make her believe her husband is heartless and callous. When you get defensive, you cooperate with evil. Valiant attempts to improve your marriage will seem dismal in your wife's eyes, if they fall short even a little. Attempting to get your wife to affirm you through your deeds alone will never work. You disarm evil when you agree with the little truth (you do make mistakes, don't you?) and you keep evil from spinning it into a larger lie (you're heartless and uncaring). All husbands will fail in caring for their wives. Your inability to get it right is not a sign that you don't care. It's actually a means of grace for you and your wife to keep looking to the Lord for help and guidance and mercy. You can see how easily it obscures God's love for you if you continue to let evil bully you toward pride and defensiveness.

Accept yourself as a man, and just a man: I regularly watch as a husband gets bullied into trying to be more than a man. Most husbands try to prove (and some even insist) they are better than they are, or they run away and hide from their failures. *It takes great strength to agree with the truth that you are just a man.* This is defiant humility. Because evil will fight so furiously against it, every husband who agrees to live honestly about his shortfalls is a strong man. Jesus felt no need to prove anything. That doesn't mean He didn't speak the truth or pick fights with the Pharisees. It just means that He followed what God called him to, even if it didn't make sense or make him look good in the moment.

God wants a husband focused on Him, not on pleasing his wife, and more dependent on His grace, not on his wife's evaluation of him. God wants His grace and mercy and truth, not the husband's performance, to be the lifeblood of the marriage. As I started to see that my effort wasn't enough to make me good or competent in my wife's eyes, I became freer to focus more on my hope and less on my performance. This degree of humility involves accepting your own limits while growing a trust and rest in God's ultimate plan of deliverance for your marriage.

This will happen as both husband and wife learn to feed on God's grace in the midst of their difficulties. The husband begins to shepherd the couple toward grace when he can comfortably admit his failures and weaknesses.

Submit to your burden: For a husband to walk into this type of change, he must learn how to let God's redemptive discipline have its work. In the flesh, evil wants men to rail against their burden (futility) in all the dangerous and destructive ways we've already seen. The redemptive way is to say, "I will not try to manage or overcome this burden, and I will not run away from it. I will let it have its work in my life. I will never get husbanding right – I will continue to make mistakes – but I will let them draw me to God so that my heart changes. I am called to care and be involved, not perform. Jesus sustains me as I freely accept my incompleteness. His words of affirmation comfort me and carry me in such a way that the futility actually softens me into a more caring man."

> Remember, it's evil you need to defy, not God and not your wife.

Stepping into this type of humility will defy evil. Submitting to the burden is not an easy step, because husbanding is such a daunting task that it either pulls on a man's desire to buck up under the pressure or forces him to run away from the challenge. I didn't want to start marriage by saying, "This is too big for me. I need help." That isn't "manly" and it certainly seemed to me at the time to be the opposite of what my wife wanted to hear. I didn't understand that one of marriage's primary gifts was that it would help me see how incomplete I was. I was used to being applauded and affirmed for being a good guy. Theoretically, I knew I was just human; I just had never had such a mirror in front of me, day in and day out, helping me see my humanity.

And it wasn't necessarily Dawn who pointed such things out. For whatever reason, my limitations became increasingly clear the longer I was married. I was set up for perfect failure. I knew only how to trust myself. The challenge in front of me beckoned me to get busy. My flesh called me toward working harder rather than toward surrender. To other men with a different past and bent, the largeness of marriage might have screamed, "Run away!" and set the bar lower. Neither path leads toward taking a humbling account of ourselves. They don't involve courageously surrendering to God's redemptive plan.

Instead of trying to quiet every sign of failure or inadequacy, a husband must bow to them, learn to ask for help from God and wait patiently for His slow deliverance. Humility says, "God, you are in charge. You have ordered things in a way I cannot resist. I will come back to You, again and again, because You are bigger than I am." God is the mighty warrior and when a husband resists the evil pull to be self-reliant, God fights for him. Instead of trying to get his wife to believe he is better than he is, or to get her to accept less, a husband must admit the truth that he is not sufficient. Then he waits for the Lord to help his wife accept this. To stand firm against evil, a husband must remember that "His pleasure is not in the strength of the horse, nor his delight in the legs of a man; the Lord delights in those who fear him, who put their hope in his unfailing love," (Psalm 147:10-11, NIV).

HELPING YOUR WIFE VOICE HER DISAPPOINTMENT

Moving into humility goes beyond the boundaries of your own heart and extends to your wife, and it's here you'll need the courage and strength and compassion you'll find from relying on the Lord. The next thing you'll aim to do is to give your wife permission to be disappointed with you. If you accept that you can't perform well enough to please your wife, you must allow her to feel and experience the discontent of living with a man who has limitations. This will ultimately be a gift to her. As you help to shepherd the focus away from your performance, she can begin to see your heart.

Take, for example, the man who thinks he's a great cook – but in fact, is not. When he continually fishes for compliments by asking his guests how they're enjoying a meal he's prepared, they feel uncomfortable because of the pressure to pretend and dance around the truth. The man's inability to be honest about himself puts everyone else in an awkward position. Similarly, when a husband has always had trouble accepting his inadequacies and finally gives his wife permission to experience and share the impact of them, she will begin to find some rest. Over time this will help her readjust her focus.

This is important: You'll need to help your wife talk about the disappointment she experiences in living with you. I suspect there will be husbands reading this who will think, "My wife already talks about that too much!" Men like that probably don't realize it, but every message they send signals that they've had enough of their wives' opinions. That makes it doubly hard for a woman to let go of her disappointment.

Because a husband is physically stronger and is more likely to turn outside the marriage for what he needs, a wife is often afraid to be straightforward with him. She doesn't want to threaten him or push him away, and because she is afraid to be honest with her husband, she tells herself, "I really can't let him know how I feel." Out of fear, she makes a conscious choice not to communicate vulnerably with her husband. She doesn't see that her martyrdom clouds her ability to recognize her everyday demeanor and the passing comments her husband does hear from her. This is part of evil's deception.

She thinks she doesn't communicate what she's feeling to her husband, but she's wrong. Instead, it comes out sideways. Her prolonged silences, or sharpness when she does speak, make it clear how she feels about her husband. Her fear keeps her blind to what she truly conveys. I've watched many marriages dissolve so far that all the wife speaks is harsh criticism, but she is so deceived and hardened by evil's lies she does not see how cruel she is being to her husband.

When a husband does not embody the courage and humility to invite his wife to talk about her disappointments, her frustration will explode in what I call a drive-by shooting. She will lob insults and explode with resentment at inappropriate times, instead of talking vulnerably about how she is hurting.

Thus, after becoming able to affirm your wife's disappointment, you're ready to develop the nerve to ask her about it and to help her to articulate it. *Part of developing understanding toward your wife means you'll need to remember that evil will regularly attack your wife to tear you and your marriage down.* This isn't because your wife lacks faith or doesn't actually believe you're a good man. It simply means your wife is vulnerable, evil has no mercy, and he often goes after her to get at your marriage.

LEARNING FROM YOUR WIFE

When a husband listens to his wife's disappointment, affirms it and helps her to articulate it, he is offering compassion and using his gifts to treat her with understanding so she can find rest. As a husband helps his wife with marital discontent, evil's deceptions will begin to fall away. In addition to helping his wife find rest, he can learn important things about himself as he listens to her. As it says in Proverbs, "Anyone who rebukes a mocker will get a smart retort. Anyone who rebukes the wicked will get hurt. So don't bother rebuking mockers; they will only hate you. But the wise, when rebuked, will love you all the more. Teach the wise, and they will be wiser. Teach the righteous, and they will learn more. Fear of the Lord is the beginning of wisdom. Knowledge of the Holy One results in understanding," (Proverbs 9:7-10).

I remember the first time my wife told me I rolled my eyes at her. I had no idea that I did that. (I probably rolled my eyes at her as she said it.) Truth be told, I had no idea I was condescending until the 1,000th time she told me so. When I finally heard her say I was condescending, I began to see that she was right. I have learned more about myself and my lack of relational holiness from my wife than from anyone else.

Because so many Christian men have misused their gifts, both as leaders in church and as husbands in marriage, they have missed glorious opportunities to discover a richer and more faith-filled obedience to the living God. The way men have shepherded in their churches and in their marriages has often meant that women are silenced. Silenced doesn't mean women don't speak. It means they are not invited to the table to be part of the conversation, and because they are not welcomed to be part of the conversation, their words often become bitter. Men seem to want to keep things running smoothly, which often grows out of their frustration with performing above the complexity and chaos they wrestle with in this fallen world. Instead of passionately being willing to make mistakes and color outside the lines, men tend to play it safe or to disengage – especially from relationship, because it is so messy. This is why women are so frequently silenced.

If they are welcomed into the conversation, I believe women can uniquely advance a fervent and courageous conformity to Christ, where like Him, our righteousness exceeds what is safe. Carolyn Custis James, a speaker and author, notes that obedience is not a matter of exactness but is actually infinite. In *The Gospel of Ruth*, she writes, "The Sermon on the Mount knocked down the walls that religious living had constructed around God's law and pointed to a way of living that goes beyond the letter of the law to the spirit. Formal religion only takes us so far – for it is both safe and doable. Love, however, knows no limits, takes costly risks, and looks for ways to give more."

She uses the example of Ruth and Boaz to illustrate this point. Ruth was a gleaner in Boaz's field. Gleaners were allowed in the field only after both teams of hired workers had finished. Ruth asked Boaz to shelve this system for her. It's as if a modern-day dumpster diver were to ask a restaurant owner to sit in his dining room and enjoy her meals for free. James says, "Boaz's response is as astonishing as Ruth's request is outrageous, and this is where our strong admiration for Boaz begins to grow. Instead of becoming defensive (this is his field, after all, and he is the boss), the lights go on and he fully embraces her suggestion. Instead of being displeased or offended, he is moved to act on her behalf. Boaz's godliness is real, and he willingly follows Ruth's lead. He actually appears driven – you might even say obsessed – to come up with ways of making her mission possible. In an astonishing outpouring of grace, Boaz exceeds the young Moabite's request."

James suggests that Ruth's asking and Boaz's supporting grow out of their cooperation with God's leadership. They worked together to advance God's purposes. Ruth was zealous in her pursuit because she cared about providing for her mother-in-law; she was moved to desire more because of relationship. Boaz responds to this and God advanced His Kingdom through them.

I stress this point because marriage is the foundation for men and women working together in the Church. It is where we practice, demonstrate, and learn about relationship between the sexes. As husbands grow the courage to listen and really hear their wives, others around them learn and grow a deeper holiness. If husbands begin to honor the voices of their wives, I believe the Church will come alive with a godliness that is much more faithful, more life-giving, and more passionate than we experience today. In her book, James puts it this way: "Walking with God takes us into a sea of possibilities that stretch our capacity for sacrifice and our imagination for obedience, reminding us there's always more to following God than we think." I can't imagine a better way to go after that than encouraging husbands to learn from their wives so the Church better reflects the way men and women can work together to advance the Gospel.

GOOD THINGS HAPPEN

As I humbly tried to move our marriage away from a focus on my performance, as I listened to Dawn and learned from her, I affirmed that she had good things to give me. It was the opposite of being proud and condescending. As I let Dawn say that I was insufficient, which early in my marriage I'd worked fervently to avoid, I experienced more freedom. I could acknowledge that I wasn't that good, I wasn't that strong, and I wasn't that capable. Now I could more comfortably walk with God and let Him help me.

More importantly, as I fearlessly learned to embody humility, I was able to help Dawn resist evil as well. The easiest way for the evil one to mock a wife's longing to participate in restorative relationship is to aggravate the burden she experiences in marriage. When I kept pressuring Dawn to affirm what a good man I was, I pushed her toward hiding, manipulating, and despairing in our relationship. However, as I used my gifts to care for her by helping her to walk through her disappointment with me, she experienced a growing freedom from the relational pain in our marriage and was invited to become a more redemptive woman. She was filled with more hope to bring life to all those in the circle of her world.

When a husband humbly accepts his inadequacies and can help his wife talk about them, he has helped her resist evil and walk in the truth. She will actually grow stronger and softer at the same time. She will be less afraid to enter into difficult relationships because she has experienced redemption with her husband, the place she experiences her burden most severely. In addition, the way her husband affirms the things she sees about him will help her hold all the other things she sees with more confidence and rest. This will help her to move toward others with discernment, kindness, and self-assurance. As a husband humbly comes alongside his wife and helps to shoulder the way she is attacked by evil, she has more strength to resist it and live out the Gospel with him and others.

9

OPENNESS

Following God as a husband is often counterintuitive. I had to grow into defiant humility; I didn't start there. It is a large step to accept your limitations as a husband and it really gets you going on the way toward Common Ground. But you still need to walk farther along your redemptive path before you can become understanding and sacrificial from a deeper place in your heart. Why? Because facing daily futility in caring for your wife will cause conflict in your inner world.

Most often I have seen the futility of marriage cause a husband to feel guilty, become angry at himself or his wife, or just find himself getting all too easily frustrated. These are natural reactions in a fallen world, but not ones that will help him follow his calling. He needs help when he reacts like this, because it gets in the way of caring for his wife. Instead, though, a husband usually tries harder or withdraws from his wife, which only intensifies his guilt, anger, frustration – or all three.

To move toward Common Ground, a husband has to take another step that's also counterintuitive. He must develop openness – an ability to receive care and ministry from the Lord – that refreshes and sustains him and gives him strength to resist the lies and attacks from the evil one. God will "strengthen those who have tired hands, and encourage those who have weak knees," (Isaiah 35:3).

And when he's struggling in his marriage, a man is tired and discouraged. He won't naturally look for help – especially help that is relational – until his heart hurts enough that it's his only option. Defiant humility uncovers the performance that hides your heart, but openness moves you toward letting God restore your heart so you have something to give your wife. "He comforts us in all our troubles so that we can comfort others. When others are troubled, we will be able to give them the same comfort God has given us," (2 Corinthians 1:4). As you learn to open up to the Lord when marriage is difficult, you can begin to let the Lord soothe your internal struggles so that you, in turn, will have comfort to offer your wife.

GUILT

A husband feels guilty when he causes a rift in his relationship with his wife, when he has hurt his wife or when his wife is struggling. Because of the everyday closeness of marriage, this often means he feels plagued by guilt pretty much all the time. Like Adam, men are trained to escape guilt in marriage by hardening to its existence, either by hiding from it or blaming it on someone else. Prior to marriage, when guilt started piling up around a relationship, guys bolted. When friendships got tough, they just stopped hanging out, or they found new friends who were more fun. Thus, going into marriage, men have little experience managing feelings of guilt in an ongoing relationship.

Most Christian men know that Christ's forgiveness matters and should help them with their guilt. But it's often hard for husbands to accept this, because they keep seeing the impact of their shortcomings on their wives. They might hear the Lord saying, "I forgive you and I am with you," but because their wives continue hurting or are irritated or scared by their behavior, Christ's forgiveness doesn't mean much to a husband and can't penetrate him very deeply. The wife's disappointment is too deafening.

When a husband follows a path of openness, he begins to admit he can't do life on his own and needs help. This is important because a husband's guilt will only be silenced if he learns to hear and accept God's grace. Your wife's affirmation will not silence your guilt; you need more than that, and wives are not designed to take God's place.

> You need more than your wife's affirmation. Wives are not designed to take God's place.

You have to learn to hear God's kindness above your wife's ongoing disappointment. You must learn to hear something your wife is not able to say to you. You need to hear God say, "Well done. You are changing and growing." Many men hear it like this: "I know you care about your wife. She does not have to affirm the genuineness of your efforts and desire to care for her. Trust me. As you rest in hearing me say, 'Well done,' and keep enduring in your marriage, you will soften and change even more. You will gain strength to communicate grace to your wife and wait with her until she can affirm who you are more clearly."

The longer husbands endure in marriage, the more God's grace becomes necessary. It really brings a man face-to-face with something he has long needed but never truly valued. This is a great gift to men that marriage can help them find. God is kind and merciful and men need His kindness, but a man often doesn't start thirsting for it until he is stricken by his wife's inability to accept him.

When Paul told me to "stand your ground, putting on the sturdy belt of truth and the body armor of God's righteousness," (Ephesians 6:14), I had no idea how much my heart would be attacked through my wife's disappointment. I had no idea how much courage it would take to believe that as a husband I stood on Christ's righteousness and not my own abilities. I had to become more open and more receptive to be impacted by God's grace. Over a long period of time I had to keep hearing Jesus affirm me before I could rest in it.

Evil wants a husband to get his significance and validation of his masculinity from his wife. A husband's definition of masculinity almost always includes a wife who cheers for him, louder and louder with each passing year. Even as he begins to listen for God's encouragement, he wants his wife to create a shortcut for him. I've done enough marital counseling to watch this theme play out again and again. I often help the husband get moving into change and he begins to relate to his wife with more kindness and strength. As he does, he wants his wife to affirm it. But it's very rare that a wife has the depth of mercy to affirm this change early in the process, because built-up resentment and bitterness will trip her up. She may feel and see some of the changes but affirming it out loud involves a level of spiritual strength few wives posses. If they're not careful, they become tense again, because he's looking for applause that she can't give. Remember, in the midst of actually doing better and changing, a husband must learn to look beyond his wife and to the Lord instead.

As a husband steps into openness by learning to be nourished by God's mercy, he can begin to feel accepted by the Lord and is less owned by that ongoing sense of guilt. The purpose of a husband's insufficiency is to bring him into deeper fellowship with Jesus. It is to get him beyond his performance to the place where God's grace is what matters most to him. As he begins to hear Jesus say, "You will never be the savior of this marriage. I ordered things that way so you would need Me more than you need her. As you see Me, as you start trusting My acceptance and affirmation of who you are in such a way that your guilt is not so debilitating, then you will be on the way to freedom." Each husband must grow the openness to hear the Lord say, "Well done!" more regularly in a way that surprises him. It often surprises him because his guilt can be so overwhelming.

Most husbands and wives believe that if a husband would pay more attention to his wife and work hard at relating to her, the marriage would get better. Instead, a husband must open up to and learn to depend on *God's* care for him. God's acceptance and love for him is a much surer anchor for a husband than trying to deal with his guilt by paying attention to his wife and working harder to please *her*. In the process of gradual growth, learning to hear "Well done," from the Lord more regularly is what will help a husband pay better attention to his wife and relate to her with more kindness.

CONTEMPT

As ongoing marital struggles persist, a husband often gets caught up in shaming himself or blaming his wife for the ongoing difficulties they encounter. When a couple goes through adversity, evil blankets them with contempt. He ridicules them so they feel ashamed about the hardship and then pushes them to assume responsibility to fix or stop it. If he can put them on the defensive, then they will blame themselves or others when they encounter rough patches. In times of adversity, evil wants people to focus on themselves or others so that they don't look to God, cry out to Him, or wait for Him to deliver them.

Evil especially loves for a husband to have contempt toward any of his wife's discontentedness. For example, couples often disagree about the level of involvement they should have with their children. In general, mothers stress how much needs to be done for the kids and want to provide direction, insight or discipline. On the other hand, fathers will often have a more "hands-off" approach. Thus, when a child gets in trouble the wife is quick to point out what could have been done to prevent the difficulty (often with an emphasis on what Dad could have done). There are certainly instances where a dad's passivity is really hurting the children, but there are just as many moms who are so controlling that their children rarely get to suffer natural consequences when they make mistakes. And even when children are properly guided, they'll still run into problems.

However, many husbands easily go on the defensive when there's a problem with the kids. In the wake of the wife's dissatisfaction the husband begins to focus on mistakes he made, or the mistakes he thinks his wife made. In his passion to prevent his wife's discontent he turns toward contempt, either at himself or at her. In both responses the husband's contempt is fueled by the couple's belief that childrearing should go smoothly, and if it doesn't, they've done something wrong.

When a couple gets in a difficult situation, they often choose to agree with the contempt evil loves to spew at them. People naturally seek to place blame. However, life in a fallen world will always mean unplanned difficulties, no matter how hard you try to avoid them. If a husband and wife continue to believe that they should not have problems or think that they should be able to easily solve them, they will always find themselves on the defensive. This provokes contempt, which will almost always be heightened in the husband. The harder he tries to improve himself or his wife, and the more he doesn't succeed, the more he will cast blame. It's a never-ending trap.

Evil wants a husband to keep thinking he can or should make it all better.

The simplest way for a husband to defuse contempt is to hear what the Lord often says in the midst of hardship: "Do not be afraid." The most-often-asked question in the Scriptures is, "How long, oh Lord?" and His most-often-repeated answer is, "Do not be afraid." In suffering or hardship, God wants it to be natural for you to call out to Him so He can comfort your fears. However, evil wants you to curl up into yourselves as he wraps you in contempt. This is where a husband's gifts come into play because his extra buoyancy means he can lift his countenance and hear the Lord say, "Do not be afraid," just a little more clearly than his wife.

Instead of contempt, a wife's flesh often tilts her toward despair and fear of the future. Because of her vulnerability in the world, a woman will often be more afraid for her safety and well-being. *In difficulty, a wife picks at her husband or is let down by him because she believes their day-to-day life would be much better if he were more competent. She doesn't realize it's often her fear of the future that is causing the pain in that moment.* Instead of putting what her husband has done in context, a wife is listening to evil tell her, "Your husband's mistakes right now are placing your future in jeopardy."

If a husband lets his wife's anxiety over the future define their relationship, his contempt will remain oversized. Again, God's care is the key to freedom in this area. Similar to his battle with guilt, a husband has to learn how to hear God say that he and his wife have a future despite the trouble they are experiencing in the moment. As a husband finds the courage to rely on God's hope, even though his wife's anguish will mock it, he is walking them toward Common Ground.

Acting like he believes what God says about them and their future will help him communicate this to his fearful wife: "Jesus' words of hope have helped soften me. We are never going to be good enough to avoid hardship. Despite ongoing difficulty, He has helped me see we have a hope and a future and I want you to learn to see it too. I could even help you learn to rest in hope, so you are not so owned by your fear. The futility and heartache we experience isn't because I don't care. I love you and care about you, but I can't always demonstrate that perfectly. As you begin to hear the Lord more clearly, you will recognize that you are not as alone as you think you are. You will start to have some hope the future might be better than you can see right now. However, to let go of your fear, you have to become more vulnerable and accept the fact that this world is not safe and it is not always my fault."

FRUSTRATION

Becoming more open to God's care helps a husband handle his frustration, the annoyance he feels at being hindered or criticized. Evil will push a husband to believe that his wife should never disagree with him, or present an obstacle he doesn't understand. How easily are some husbands irritated by their wives?

In general, husbands are set up for an inordinate amount of frustration because of the way they are raised. As a boy is guided into being a man, he is routinely "fathered" by the prince of this world instead of by God. Whether it's in the way a boy is cared for at home, at school, in sports, or by what he hears through books and the media, he will not be consistently touched with the compassion and tenderness that will help him turn away from frustration. For a husband to grow out of the irritation that plagues him in marriage, he must change from being defined by the way this world has raised him and respond to God's parenting. Only as a man lets God father him can he become an understanding husband.

Consider this theme in the realm of a father-son relationship. "For our earthly fathers disciplined us for a few years, doing the best they knew how. But God's discipline is always right and good for us because it means we will share in his holiness," (Hebrews 12:10). As hard as earthly fathers try to be good, they are really nothing like what children really need. There are only three direct imperative commands that speak to the parent-child relationship in the New Testament epistles. Two of them address the way fathers treat their children: "Fathers, don't aggravate your children. If you do, they will become discouraged and quit trying," (Colossians 3:21); later Paul writes, "Now a word to you fathers. Don't make your children angry by the way you treat them," (Ephesians 6:4).

If I were going to summarize biblical advice to fathers raising sons, I would say, "Realize that evil will always want your son to be upset by the intricacies of life. Your ability to be patient and involved in his life will be a taste of God's kindness to him. This will help give him composure as he faces difficulties, and he won't be as easily frustrated. This will be the very thing that will start him off in a good direction as a husband." As a father represents God's kindness, his son will have an easier time remembering, "The LORD is like a father to his children, tender and compassionate to those who fear him," (Psalm 103:13)

As a husband begins to open up to God as his father, he allows the frustrations of life to turn him toward God for help. There is no way I could recall the number of anguishing conversations I have had with God since becoming a husband. What should have felt like pained difficulty that I naturally brought to the Lord felt like extreme frustration that I thrust at Him. Marriage represented complication to me in a way that nothing ever has and I couldn't run away from it. It frustrated me. However, the more I shared that disturbance with God, the less Dawn had to get. *My frustration softened as I grew the courage to start praying it to God.*

I imagine it might seem weird to read that "praying your frustration to God" is courageous, but I think it is. The Scriptures make it clear that the fleshly nature is self-serving and hostile toward God. Therefore, in your flesh, it is natural to remove your responsibility and blame God in frustration.

For instance, when I am counseling a man who turns to pornography as a way to soothe his ache, I try to help him see his fleshly annoyance. At times I might say, "When you turn to pornography after a fight with your wife, it is a way to act out in anger toward her and God." I suggest that his actions say to his wife and God, "Neither of you understands me or take cares of me the way I need, so I'll just take care of myself!" I always suggest that it's better for a man to speak that frustration directly to God than for him to let it come out sideways through lustful acts.

People often aren't able to admit their fleshly irritation with God. But until you can relate honestly with God, you will not be able to move into an essential stage of your relationship with Him – the depth of sanctification that brings you closer to Him here on earth.

Here's how it works. Your fleshly nature creates a practical distance between you and God. Sanctification happens when you begin to be conscious of letting your human impulses and fleshly nature die away, instead listening for God's voice and God's will to become reconciled to Him. Your flesh is crucified, or diminished, and as a result you experience an increasing closeness with the Lord.

How can this happen? One way is by being willing to come before Him with all your pain and frustrations and anger. You lament. It's an old-fashioned-sounding word, but lamenting (praying openly and honestly) is a critical element in setting aside your flesh in order to achieve openness and sanctification.

First of all, lamenting is different than grumbling. Grumbling is blaming God for your disenchantment and moving away from Him. Lamenting is bringing your frustration to God and pouring it all out to Him, with genuine faith that He will still love you when all is said and done. The two postures are close, and yet worlds apart.

We've lost the art of lamenting. Instead, most men fall apart by getting angry or giving up when they run into difficulties. Remember, evil has convinced them life was never supposed to be so hard, right? And that they should be able to tough it out on their own, right? The evil one wants to reinforce a husband's need to maintain a stiff upper lip. To keep cool. To stay in control. Trouble is, the longer he keeps that up and refuses to go before God with his pain and anger and fear, the more he'll turn his frustrations upon his wife. You already know where that leads.

Husbands are ill-equipped to care for their wives because they have not opened themselves up to the deep care of a gracious and merciful Father. The deep frustration I felt in marriage for many years brought me face-to-face with a Father who would not – and could not – turn away from me.

God uses marriage to father a husband. Having a "thorny" wife is the perfect reminder that you need Someone bigger to help you. I poured my frustration out to God and complained to Him. Sometimes, I even insinuated that His grand idea of staying married to the same person forever was really not that wise. I lamented to Him they way David and Job did – I said things that were not nice. He accepted my immaturity and loved me through it. He never backed away from me and never acted like I was too much. Instead, He loved me. That unnerving love, which I clearly didn't deserve, changed my frustration and grew in me something I could give my wife. As God humbly fathered me, I became a husband.

GOODNESS

The Scriptures clearly teach the reality of reciprocal care. We give what we have received from God. God's care for me – in the midst of guilt, condemnation and frustration – sustained and changed me so I could give to Dawn what I received from Him.

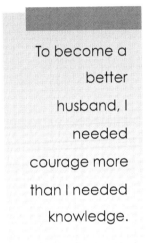

To become a better husband, I needed courage more than I needed knowledge.

Frequently, when I am encouraging a husband to be more present to his wife, I hear him protest, "But I don't know what I'm doing." He thinks he lacks knowledge, and that's the reason he's unable to make himself more available to care about her world. He makes the assumption that because I'm a counselor, I *do* know what to do. My training as a counselor certainly helps me to be an encouragement to others, but I grew most as a counselor and as a man when I kept having the nerve to sit down with Dawn and welcome what was going on with her. Earlier in marriage, I'd always withdrawn from Dawn or tried to control her, mostly because I was afraid of what was going on inside of her. To become a better husband, I needed courage more than I needed knowledge.

It may sound crazy, but trying to carry my wife's burdens by listening to and shouldering the evil that was harassing her meant my life became more conflicted. It took extreme bravery to keep feeding on the tenderness and compassion Jesus offered me in the times I poured out my heart to Him. Evil was trying to beat me down with guilt, contempt, and frustration as I tried to care for Dawn. As I persevered and God's grace strengthened me, I changed inside and was kinder to Dawn.

As a husband opens up and more actively depends on the Lord to be his comforter and defender, the evil one will not be as free in the marriage. Like every husband, you want your wife to affirm that you are a good man, but it is more important that you learn to hear this from the Lord. As you do, it will help you grow the type of goodness your wife will have a hard time ignoring.

10

GENEROUS INVOLVEMENT

An uninvolved husband takes on different outward forms. The gruff, drill sergeant-type husband seems perpetually irate. When his wife wants him to build a deck on the back of the house, he does. But as he works, he lets her know he's irritated. He'd rather be on the couch watching football. He makes quick, demeaning comments, many under his breath, because he's been asked to sacrifice some time and effort to please his wife. He has no idea he is relating that way. Instead, he prides himself on a job well done, thinking that his effort ought to translate into both attention and adulation from his wife. He's genuinely shocked (and angered) when she fails to respond as he expects and requires.

On the other end of the scale rests the shy, uncertain man. This husband doesn't build the deck; he hires someone to do it, partially because he's sure his wife doesn't believe he's up to the job. When the handyman finishes the job weeks late and way over budget, he writes the check under a cloud of shame. When his wife questions the cost overruns, he mumbles something and walks away, remaining cold and distant for a couple of days until his wife apologizes for being insensitive. This husband controls his wife through childlike docility.

The drill sergeant husband doesn't *appear* weak, because he is so controlling. But his frustrated, short-tempered way of relating says he does not have the strength to involve himself patiently with others. Those in relationship with him must perform for him, because he can't handle real relationship. The diffident man has covered his pride. People who know him in passing would call him a "nice guy," but that niceness is a mask for his pride. He's not really ever needed God, because he's never taken any chances. His safe approach to life has caused his inner man to atrophy. He does not possess the strength to initiate anything, instead manipulating others into coming through for him. He's placed his pride before his trust in God by saying, "My plan is better than Yours. Your plan involves taking chances and facing failure. I am too obstinate for that. I would rather cause people to feel anxious in my presence so they feel the need to take care of me."

Both husbands have been too proud to let God mature them and are owned by relationship inexperience, futility, selfishness and spiritual attack. When a husband lets these obstacles own him, he is too shut down to really engage his wife. In such a husband's world, the flesh has deceived him so subtly that following it has become a way of life. Evil has won.

The drill sergeant husband will actually say his wife lacks compliance, which is why he's required to be so tough. He is so blind that he cannot recognize he's crippled her with fear; she will do almost anything he says just to protect herself. The passive man says, "My wife is just so busy. It doesn't matter what I do." He has no idea how much busier she needs to become in the presence of his weakness. How these husbands choose to define their wives simply evolves from the lies they have chosen to believe – not from what's actually true.

Proverbs has a word for this kind of uninvolved husband: a sluggard. Consider this: "The sluggard says, 'There is a lion in the road, a fierce lion roaming the streets!' " (Proverbs 26:13, NIV). He remains uninvolved because of his fear – the imaginary lion. There's no lion out in the street. That's the deception that allows him to keep his wife at arm's length. A sluggard will always find some imaginary reason to justify his lack of participation with her. This pleases evil, because a sluggard is never available to come to his wife's defense.

A GENEROUS MAN

On the other hand, "The soul of the sluggard craves and gets nothing, while the soul of the diligent is richly supplied," (Proverbs 13:4, ESV). A man who endures through the difficulty of marriage while holding onto the Lord – or letting the Lord hold onto him – becomes fruitful because he has a rich soul. He has a storehouse of inner character he can lavish on his wife. He is what the psalmist calls a generous man.

A generous man mocks evil because he's gained understanding and maturity. He knows that the great obstacles in front of him need not cause him to shrivel up inside. Instead, he lets his difficulties drive him to the Lord. *He goes deeper into the Gospel, which frees him to grow a generosity of person – he gives more of himself.*

Psalm 112 expresses praise for a glorious man, describing him also as a generous man. Life "goes well for those who are generous, who lend freely... They give generously to those in need." Three times his generosity is mentioned as an admirable quality. To hear this compliment in the correct context, you must remember that in the Old Testament, righteousness was understood in more outward terms –

like wealth, land, and safety – than in the New Testament. God was doing something more visible in the Old Testament. He was establishing an earthly representation of what He would do through the eventual unfolding of His full purposes. Therefore, outward things, like what he owned and how he was a steward of those possessions, were seen to reflect a man's godliness. In the New Testament, God's work is less visible and man demonstrated his generosity by his love of God and his neighbor.

Consider what a generous husband looks like today. He has an abundance of inward character to lavish upon his wife, a storehouse of understanding, steadfastness, compassion, grace, truth, discernment, and courage. He is not holding all of himself in because evil has shut him down; he is mocking evil by lavishing who he is on those he loves. Ecclesiastes, which is all about how to deal with the mystery of life through faith, says this: "Give generously, for your gifts will return to you later. Divide your gifts among many, for you do not know what risks might lay ahead," (Ecclesiastes 11:1-2). A godly man has made some peace with futility and knows the way to deal with it is not to become cautious and protective of his heart, but to risk and give all that is inside of him as he loves like God.

> A generous husband mocks evil by lavishing who he is on those he loves.

To this man, evil is no longer a bully. He isn't afraid. He knows the evil one will rob, kill and destroy, but he also knows that God is a master at making man's feeble efforts into more. He has looked at his weaknesses face-to-face so they no longer scare him. He has given his wife permission to talk about them and has found an irresistible love that gives him strength in the midst of a chaotic world.

COMPASSION

For the lies of evil to have less hold on a wife, a husband must grow the courage to welcome his wife's weaknesses with a compassion that disarms her.

As a husband awakens to the sin and fallen-ness that surrounds his marriage, he usually wants to do something about it. But often he either moves with brute force or he doesn't move at all. Moving in love comes from compassion. This is why a husband must first grow humility and openness. When he's come to understand that he fails his wife and he's learned to receive ministry from the Lord, he can move toward her out of genuine compassion and not obligation.

In the parable of the Good Samaritan, Jesus says, "Then a despised Samaritan came along, and when he saw the man, he felt deep pity. Kneeling beside him, the Samaritan soothed his wounds with medicine and bandaged them," (Luke 10:33-34). In this passage, the Greek word for compassion is a strong word that brings to mind a full-bodied response. It was like the Samaritan had a gut-wrenching reaction and had no choice but to help the wounded man. The priest and the Levite had already passed by, unmoved.

The Samaritan's response was a direct contradiction to the reaction of the religious leaders. Jesus is getting at something here. He suggests that the religious men showed their true, hard hearts, perpetuating injustice by walking past a wounded soul who was right in front of them. If a husband has genuinely begun to grow humility and openness, it will be harder for him to walk right by his hurting wife. A husband does not discover biblical love by being told what to do or by being held accountable. He finds it through repentance. Genuine inner change gives both the sight and the compassion to move *toward* those in need.

Jesus was moved to heal the sick because He felt compassion for them (Matthew 14:14) and He was moved by compassion to begin teaching the crowds because they seemed like sheep without a shepherd (Mark 6:34). In the same way, when a husband is genuinely moved by compassion to care about his wife, he helps to wash the lies of evil away from her.

COURAGE

The generous involvement a mature husband lavishes on his wife actually grows out of courage, because this is the point when he starts to go toe-to-toe with evil. When David said, "Don't worry about a thing. I'll go fight this Philistine!" (1 Samuel 17:32), it had nothing to do with what he saw in himself or who he thought he was. His assurance in the presence of Goliath was something much bigger than he could manufacture. He said, "I have been taking care of my father's sheep. When a lion or a bear comes to steal a lamb from the flock, I go after it with a club and take the lamb from its mouth. If the animal turns on me, I catch it by the jaw and club it to death. I have done this to both lions and bears, and I'll do it to this pagan Philistine, too, for he has defied the armies of the living God! The Lord who saved me from the claws of the lion and the bear will save me from this Philistine," (1 Samuel 17:34-37). David's courage was borne out of relationship with the living God. He knew Who had his back, and it gave him courage.

Consider a Proverb that affirms courage: "The wicked run away when no one is chasing them, but the godly are as bold as lions," (Proverbs 28:1). Evil loves to bully weak husbands and he often uses wives to do it. Evil gets a wife tied up in all sorts of angst so that her husband just runs away. Imagine the power, on the other hand, if a husband were to pick up his sword and say, "Evil, you're not that big. You're certainly no match for the mighty warrior who lives in and through me."

In the early years of our marriage I felt like I gave a lot. It sure seemed easy, mostly because I was following my flesh and my motivation was twisted. What I thought of as generosity, it turns out, had one of two basic goals – either to make me look good or to get Dawn off my back. It was easy to recognize the lack of love in my "gifts," because if Dawn wasn't moved, I sulked or got mad.

Much later in the marriage, I found I could give to Dawn and it mattered less whether I got any credit. At the same time, evil mocked me more significantly because genuine giving had the power to touch Dawn much more deeply. Everything slowed down and felt more arduous and shaky. *Giving to Dawn became harder as I grew in maturity, because evil was fighting against it more vigorously.* You can almost see it as a scripted swordfight, except for one thing. Evil never plays by the script.

TRUTH

It takes even more faith and courage for a husband to become truthful with his wife because evil so often perpetrates deceit in her heart. This may sound strange, but I often know a man is growing the courage to enter into the deepest part of Satan's territory in marriage when he can actually say, "My wife hurt me." I don't mean he's speaking like a wounded little boy, but like a husband calmly sharing with his precious wife, "I have realized that you sin just like me. You are so focused on wanting me to get better that you can't see that you hurt me in the same way I hurt you. It just looks different to you."

For a man to step between evil and his wife, he must have clear vision that she cooperates with evil at times and that this cooperation is sometimes aimed at him. He must see and feel that his wife's sin truly impacts

120

him. Many husbands choose to believe things like, "My wife is way more spiritual than me," or, "She loves the Lord so much. One day I hope I can be like her." Your wife is no more perfect than you are, so stop being naive.

There is no wife who has not sinned meaningfully against her husband. Until he can feel and see it, he won't have the courage to help her see it as well. If you can see your wife's sin and understand how it impacts you, you'll want to begin to help her with it. And helping a wife see her sin, actually uncovering it for her, means a man will have to engage the one who has lied to her.

Please remember I am encouraging this direction *after* defiant humility and openness. Those paths form compassion that helps you to speak truth in love. For many years I spoke "truth" that was not true because it was not expressed lovingly. I needed to start living a life that was more defined by defiant humility and openness. Only then was I was prepared to speak truth that was seasoned in love.

This first time I ever felt myself doing this well could just as easily have swung another direction. It was a potential perfect storm – the episode involved our girls and their safety, and after three weeks passed Dawn still wasn't over what had happened. Here's how it went:

One Saturday morning, our girls came bounding in the front door after being out playing in the neighborhood. My oldest, Aimee, walked past her mom and came straight to me. She said, "We want to go get some pizza with our friends. Can you give us some money so we can go with them?" The pizza place was less than a mile's walk from our house, but they'd never been off on their own before. I was a little nervous about letting them go, since they were pre-teens and the oldest friends were only 14. But it sounded fun, and I had confidence in them. So I gave Aimee some money and a little advice, and they were on their way.

About 45 minutes later Dawn announced she was going running. (She wasn't really going running. She was going to check on the girls while wearing running clothes. But I played along.) By the time she got to the pizza place, the kids were gone. Dawn hadn't seen them on the way there, and she didn't see them on the way home. It turns out the girls had gone into a shop right next door to the restaurant for some dessert to eat on the walk home, but Dawn didn't know that. She was a wreck. To tell you the truth, I had no idea how nervous Dawn felt about the whole outing. As a father, I liked the sense of adventure and how the girls were exploring their independence. It just made Dawn feel afraid.

Three weeks later Dawn came to me and said, "We need to have a discussion and I think it's going to be an argument."

I couldn't imagine what was on her mind.

She said, "You know exactly want I want to talk about. It's about you letting our girls go to that pizza place. I think you are reckless with our kids and I don't think you have their best interests at heart."

I said, "Honey, I'm willing to re-think that decision. But I really don't think you believe that I am reckless with our kids and that I don't have their best interests at heart."

This led to a long, painful, but self-controlled conversation. I tried to help Dawn see that she was speaking partially out of panic, because it was the first time our girls had ever gone unsupervised out in the world. What surprised me most was that I did not get angry and defensive. I had let Dawn talk so often about my weaknesses that I had little to be defensive about. I was listening to learn, and I had also become open enough with the Lord that He was giving me buoyancy in that discussion so I was able to resist evil. My pride didn't get riled up, so I could let Dawn say whatever she needed to say and I didn't feel compelled to attack her back. I talked with Dawn, I listened to her, and I tried to help her see that in some ways the whole situation had aroused her flesh as a mother. In the weeks that had ensued she had focused on those fears and built a case against me as a husband and father. She spoke to me out of that terror. For the first time in our married life I felt like I patiently helped her without being rough, condescending, or distant. We stayed in the conversation and learned a lot, instead of becoming more divided.

A husband who is growing a "generosity of person" by lavishing grace helps to create an atmosphere where his wife can come alive and trust him. As that happens, he can embody the Gospel more directly and speak into his wife's inner chaos, which is fostered by the deceptions of evil. He can help her see her unbelief and sinful patterns while also encouraging her to see where Jesus is working and transforming her into more of Himself.

As a husband grows a generous involvement, he can be part of a more direct engagement in the way evil is attacking her. For a wife to become more beautiful on the inside – for her faith to grow – two things have to happen. She needs to taste His grace and she needs to hear His truth; a generous husband can grow the inner character to be a vehicle that embodies these qualities.

BASE CAMP: A WIFE'S CALLING

The Gospel calls a husband to sacrifice and understanding. His calling points a husband beyond his human frailties and failings. It moves him toward a heart change that life empowered by the Holy Spirit can bring. Unfortunately, the husband's biblical calling can get disrupted at every turn, sometimes even by the words we use to describe him. Calling him the leader or the decision-maker and putting the "power" in his hands alone, without recognizing his wife's participation, threatens to energize his sinful, prideful nature and encourage the division evil is trying to establish.

In addition, such terms tend to diminish the wife's role in fighting evil alongside her husband. Working toward a redemptive marital atmosphere is not the husband's responsibility alone. If we're saying that marriage is a bit like climbing a mountain, you'll find richer beauty as you learn to work together and battle through the difficulties you encounter. But no one's going to make it to the top, or even very far out of base camp, if the husband's carrying all the gear and his wife is perched on top of his pack, pointing out his mistakes. So how does God mean for a wife to walk with her husband toward Common Ground?

VULNERABILITY

One of a woman's most significant contributions comes through her vulnerability. In our culture, which prizes aggression and power, this may not immediately strike you as an asset. Compare it with her husband's gifts. Typically, she is not the physically stronger of the two, nor is she hard-wired to receive validation outside the marriage in the same way her husband does.

Our society has come to view vulnerability as interchangeable with weakness, but I ask you to reconsider. Consider the often-used image of the graceful willow that bends but is not broken in winds that topple mighty but rigid oaks. A wife's vulnerability is rooted in that same gentle, yielding endurance.

This vulnerability is deeply entwined with a wife's calling, and like her husband's, will feel deeply counterintuitive. Women since the days of Eve have been deeply burdened by relational pain. Yet the directives from the New Testament call wives to meet such pain head-on and endure under its weight.

Essentially, God says to women, "There will be no husband good enough to keep you from needing Me. If you learn to let your husband's frailties and failures push you toward a deeper trust in Me, you will most likely find more love with your husband. But if you do not let your marital difficulties push you toward Me, you will miss the joy of that redemptive love." God's burden actually invites a wife to a much deeper faith.

AWE

Paul writes, "The wife must respect her husband," (Ephesians 5:33). But don't simply take this to mean that a wife is to have high esteem for the man she married and, and as a result, do everything he says. *No husband can perform that well and no wife should pretend that much.*

We want to believe that marriage is easy and clean. But that minimizes the pain that comes in such an intimate relationship, and it oversimplifies what happens in a marriage. There will always be times when a husband is too selfish, when his behavior forces his wife to question him and his love. There will always be times a wife will need to endure this kind of relational challenge.

When you view a husband under the lens of biblical love, *every* man falls short of what he is called to be as a husband. No man is good enough to treat his wife lovingly at all times. He will not always be able to earn her respect and no wife should have to live so naively as to always think well of her husband.

In this context, respecting her husband means a wife is to grow a reverential fear toward him. This is similar to the "fear of the Lord" mentioned in other passages of scripture, and it's not the same thing as being afraid. You don't fear the Lord because He has the power to strike you down; you stand back in wonder that He lived and died for you and perseveres in caring for you.

Having a reverential fear of your husband does not mean you should ever cower before him. It means you stand in awe that he's willing to endure through relationship carelessness, worldly futility, selfishness, and spiritual attack to grow patiently into generous involvement with you, as he does his best to model the relationship Christ has with His Church.

A wife doesn't grow respect for her husband because he always cares for her well. She certainly doesn't respect him because he always gets it right. *Biblical respect from a wife is an awe-inspired appreciation that her husband doesn't give up, despite the fact that he has to battle through so much to become loving and understanding.* When a wife is willing to consider what her husband endures, it helps soften the pain of her disappointments and fuels her desire to wait for and encourage him.

A wife generally asks a great deal from her husband, and can be oblivious to how much she accepts evil's lies. Evil goads her to dwell upon her husband's failures, causing her to become dissatisfied with him and with their marriage. This diminishes her beauty. The spiritual atmosphere around her becomes agitated, making it harder for her husband to move toward her. As her needs and wishes get tangled up with evil's lies, it becomes easier for her to shame her husband with insults or by withdrawing from him when he doesn't perform up to her expectations.

Respect is a gift a wife offers when she fights through her resentment and evil's lies, and then acknowledges what her husband goes through to care for her. *When a wife recognizes how easily her flesh is inflamed by her husband's weaknesses, she will see how respecting him helps oppose evil.* As she realizes the intensity of what he faces, it helps them resist evil together. This is a wife who is growing an awe-inspired appreciation for her husband. She says, "You mean my husband keeps trying to battle against his tendency to be selfish? He keeps standing up to his fears and his lack of know-how and his cluelessness over how to take care of me, and refuses to give up? This man has the faith to keep believing that God can transform his faltering efforts into a love for me. The fact that he keeps moving through his frustration is a holy thing!" When a wife grows that type of inner beauty, it speaks powerfully to her husband.

Dawn and I had no idea how this theme would play out in our own marriage. I naturally tried hard to please her and thought she would be stunned by my goodness. My pride and desire for her to affirm me overwhelmed her. Slowly, as I grew into seeing my insecurity and pride, I was genuinely broken by its impact on Dawn. This helped things begin to soften, but Dawn still had a flood of memories of how I had acted in difficult periods that were hard to get past even as we were moving toward something better. *Evil incites division by haunting a wife with memories of a husband's past mistakes so she misses the genuineness of her husband's current efforts.* In the moment, her lack of respect often grows out the battle in her mind to put her husband's efforts in the context of their whole marital journey.

As I slowly changed, Dawn began to get a deeper sense of awe at my faithfulness, and she began to fight evil by giving her respect as a gift. This gift said to me, "I see you and know that you are fighting so much. I will battle resentment and despair and appreciate your efforts, even when they seem too small to me. My hope is that this will help you endure in your calling. We have more to celebrate together and I look forward to sharing it with you."

SUBMISSION

In addition to respecting her husband, a wife is called to submit to him. The actual New Testament directives are to "accept the authority of your husbands" (1 Peter 3:1,5) and "to submit to your husbands as you do to the Lord," (Ephesians 5:22). These words, accept and submit, mean you receive the care your husband provides – sacrificial and loving, yet fallen and flawed – and give yourself to the purpose for which it exists. You must grow an inner fortitude that helps you not only honor your husband's gifts, but more actively cooperate with his efforts to bring the two of you together (despite his inability to do this consistently well).

A husband will never shepherd a marriage perfectly, but that doesn't mean a wife can't humbly learn how to help, even when evil whispers to her that his efforts are well below his ability. As she gains this strength, she is able to "conquer evil by doing good," (Romans 12:21). She grows the faith to give her husband active kindness as a way to encourage and support him.

The word "accept" used in 1 Peter 3 is the same word "submit" that is used in Ephesians 5:22. Essentially, the word in Greek means *to arrange yourself under*. If God has given a husband gifts to love his wife, she must learn how to endure, or remain, under his imperfect care and still learn how to work together with him. Accepting and submitting means a wife continually moves back into relationship with her husband, working alongside him while learning to trust in the direction they are heading. Submission doesn't mean, "I'll do everything you say." It's more like, "I'm on your team regardless of what comes, and I will join with you because I believe in what we are trying to accomplish together."

To gain a richer understanding of biblical submission, you need to drop the negative connotation that has become attached to the concept of submission in our culture. Often, submission can be taught in a way that would remind you of a puppy's obedience training: "Sit." "Stay." "Fetch." This outlook focuses on the act – doing what you're told to do by your (we hope) loving master – rather than on the relational process. But a husband isn't a master, and people should never be asked to respond this way; we're vulnerable and need a lot of practice and help to grow into the things the Lord calls us to. Submission is a much larger and more arduous calling than rote obedience ever could be.

The New Testament teaches gradual sanctification – slow growth in Christ – and when submission is considered in that context, you recognize it is a deep, interpersonal process. It's like a relational dance, in which the wife grows into submission while her husband grows in sacrificing and caring for her. The quality of true submission between two humans grows as they mature in their respective callings.

The call to wives in 1 Peter 3 comes in the middle of a long section on submission. In this passage, Peter exhorts citizens to submit to civil authority, slaves to submit to masters (even if they are cruel), and then he includes the example of Jesus' willingness to yield to the shame of the cross in response to his Father's will. Finally Peter says, "In the same way, you wives must accept the authority of your husbands," (1 Peter 3:1).

The call to submission is revolutionary. All through history, government officials have been prone to use power unjustly. Owners weren't exactly known for their kind treatment of slaves. As Jesus followed His Father's call to go to the cross, He felt such inner turmoil that He cried out, "My God, my God, why hast Thou forsaken me?" (Matthew 27:46). What a difficult calling for a wife, to give herself to her husband *in the same way* as citizens to civil authority, as slaves to masters, as Jesus to His Father.

There is nothing easy about submission in its biblical context. Wives are asked to believe the best about men, a species that has excelled at exploiting women. Because government officials, slave owners, and husbands often have misused their advantages, Peter is underscoring the power of submission to exemplify biblical love.

In response to Jesus' gift to you on the cross, you can learn the beauty of submission and the glory of cooperating with someone who is called to serve you, but who will not always do things well. Submission often requires that you trust Jesus with your life as you allow Him to make sense of what He is asking you to do. It's not surprising that this long passage on submission occurs in an epistle about suffering, or that Peter assures us that God is pleased at our patient faith.

As a wife grows in welcoming her husband's care despite the pain it may involve, she is able to cooperate more actively with his broken efforts. For example, a husband may not understand the way his wife wants to nurture their relationship by being romantic or by decorating their home to create a more pleasant place to live. He may be too nervous to spend money on such things, instead stashing money away toward retirement. He may grumble about his wife's spending. Naturally, this wife might be disappointed in her husband's fear and hurt by his attitude, but that doesn't have to push her totally away from him.

Submission doesn't mean, "I'll do everything you say." It's more like, "I'm on your team and I believe in what we're trying to do together."

Instead, she could look to the Lord to help her grieve through aspects of her current stage in marriage. This will only enhance her spiritual sensitivity and relational wisdom so that she can give herself more discerningly to her husband and to their marriage. In doing so, she might come to see that her husband *does* care about her, but might not have the faith to demonstrate his love in the area of finances. As she stands against resentment or bitterness and unreservedly enjoys the money they do spend, while trying to help her husband loosen up, she is submitting to her husband. It's not wrong for her to hope that more will unfold, but in the meantime, she unites with her husband right where they are now.

As she learns to join her husband's efforts to bring them together, she also learns the biblical view of submission. She may not always think his efforts are what they should be, and often they won't be, but as she grows in humility she will more easily cooperate with his efforts in meaningful ways. It's hardly passive; in fact, it's one of the most active elements of a woman's calling.

RESTFULNESS

Even when a husband and wife are doing the best they can, the husband will still stumble and walk in unbelief. This can unleash a wife's fear and anxiety, prompting her to *do something*, whether that means making noise to arouse her husband or becoming extra-tame to soothe him. She just wants her husband to make it all better – fast. A wife's flesh will pull her toward both forms of relating – pushiness or acquiescence – in response to her husband's ongoing weaknesses. This will intensify evil's work, not help to disarm it.

When you are in a vulnerable position (as a wife so often is) and your husband is walking in unbelief in a way that affects you intimately, it is hard to stay at rest. In fact, it's natural to grab and claw for something that makes you feel safe and protected, rather than turn to God. When a wife keeps trying to manufacture her own solutions instead of resting in the Lord and considering whether any action is necessary, she becomes more of a distraction to her husband and his call to bring them together. Proverbs refers to this type of wife as nagging. "A nagging wife is as annoying as the constant dripping on a rainy day. Trying to stop her complaints is like trying to stop the wind or hold something with greased hands," (Proverbs 27:15-16).

As always, Scripture provides a more encouraging image to follow – the restful woman. "Her husband can trust her, and she will greatly enrich his life. *She will not hinder him but help him all her life,*" (Proverbs

31:11-12). A woman who has engaged the Gospel over a period of time grows the type of faith where she can laugh a little at the pains in this world. She wants good relationship with her husband, but is not owned by a lack of it. She practices growing fruitfulness in other areas of her life. Her world is more defined by God and His commitment to her. This is particularly important when a couple faces complex or troublesome situations and a husband's unbelief is stirred up. When a wife is filled with hope because of her connection to the Lord, she comes alive in the midst of tension and discerns how to cooperate with the Lord in the way she relates to her husband.

A wife who relates out of despair has trusted herself more than God and is usually blind to what she is doing. Her thoughts and actions are the only things that make sense to her in the moment. She will offer input, help, or suggestions whether or not they are needed. She is certain her husband can't make it without her. The more she offers herself out of desperation, the more the husband's call to follow God is obscured. The things he needs to see about himself, his God, their marriage and life are far more difficult to identify and go after.

In his epistle, Peter directly counsels women to lay their efforts and their fear at God's feet. Peter's call is radical for women whose husbands have an established relationship with God. But in the church he's addressing, many of the wives had unbelieving husbands, so this charge must have seemed nearly impossible. Yet, Peter calls them to faith and thus encourages all women, no matter the circumstances, to trust God first instead of having confidence in solutions that appear readily, or that they can manufacture themselves.

He says, "Your godly lives will speak to them better than any words. They will be won over by watching your pure, godly behavior. Don't be concerned about the outward beauty that depends on fancy hairstyles, expensive jewelry, or beautiful clothes. You should be known for the beauty that comes from within, the unfading beauty of a gentle and quiet spirit, which is so precious to God," (1 Peter 3:1-4). Peter is writing of wives who had become noisy. Their noise was verbal – they were literally talking too much – but it manifested itself in frantic activity as well. When Peter tells wives not to focus on outward beauty, he wasn't telling them to neglect their appearance. He was cautioning them against employing self-reliant means to manipulate their husbands. Whenever a wife tries to motivate her husband or draw him toward her by her own actions alone, she will actually make it harder for him to love her. This is a universal theme that gets played out in marriages again and again. In her flesh, a wife wants to do whatever she can in her own strength to help the marriage – to trust what she sees. However, God wants her to trust in Him and in what she can't see – an inner beauty and faith that only He can nurture and grow in her.

> Think more about *how* you talk to and question your husband, not *whether* you do.

Because inward beauty is achieved through gradual sanctification, an arduous and taxing journey, many women seek a more manageable shortcut. You don't have to look far. A most unscientific survey of women's magazine covers seems to bear that out. An entire segment of our society exists to make sure women feel diminished if they are not thin, well-dressed, and flawless.

Peter would say that is foolish and dangerous. He says the best way for wives to entice husbands is through inward beauty. When a woman becomes more restful inside, it amplifies her inner beauty and invites others around her to see and hear God. Her husband will need to see, hear, and reach out for more of God instead of being monopolized by his wife's temporary (and distracting) shortcuts. Peter underscores the wisdom found throughout Scripture – real power is most often inner and unseen. It is not found in position or possession. A wife who grows deep rest in Jesus and in His care for her will get the attention of her husband and help to draw him to God.

Wives, I suggest that you aim for *restfulness*. I have chosen to use this word instead of "quietness" for a reason. In my experience, Christian wives are either confused or callous about how to speak to their husbands. I want to avoid clouding the issue any further. I have witnessed wives who believe they should never question their husbands, because that is not being "quiet." I have also watched wives who give no thought to what they say or how they say it, in part because the concept of "quietness" has been used as a means to marginalize them. Neither extreme is healthy; every couple has to create a humble atmosphere in which they can speak and listen to each other to help uncover their blind spots.

In fact, I know that as I lay out my thoughts they can easily be misconstrued and come to mean that a wife should remain quiet and passive regardless of what her husband does. I hope that by the way I speak to both husbands and wives, and by the examples I use, I make it clear that a husband needs his wife to be strong enough to help reveal his sin. In grave situations such as domestic violence, a wife must clearly take action to protect herself. As I introduce the concept of restfulness to couples, I'm addressing the ways a husband and wife build a redemptive relationship. A wife's fleshly tendency is to become more "noisy" or to manipulate her husband, instead of resting in the Lord. This is what she needs help to believe and trust, in general terms.

So, when Peter says what will really impact a husband is the "unfading beauty of a gentle and quiet spirit," he is telling wives that their deepest hope lies not in their activity, but in their trust in God as the author of life and redemption. As they rest in Him, He will care for them and through them to bring redemption to their marriage. You can talk with your husband and even question him, but your words should flow out of confidence and rest in God's care for you. Think more about *how* you talk to and question your husband, not *whether* you do. Every husband should grow the humility to listen to his wife and every wife should grow the ability to communicate with her husband. Humble, redemptive conversation is the goal.

ENDURING WELL

When Peter says that the unfading beauty of a gentle and quiet spirit is precious to God, he is really saying two things at once. Through the inspiration of the Holy Spirit, Peter is saying God loves for a woman to really change on the inside because it is the best way for her to impact those in the circle of her life. He is also saying that the Lord jealously desires deeper communion with every wife. As the difficulty in marriage forces her to go deeper with Him, He is pleased. Women get married to have a human companion, not realizing their desire for this relationship will compel them to trust more in God. As her marital troubles cause a wife to reach out for more of Jesus, her inner transformation begins. Her eyes will be opened to how much she has trusted in herself more than in the Lord.

If marriage helps a wife to look more to Jesus, she will find His help. He, too, learned to be faithful in the midst of difficulty and rejection. Right before Peter addresses the calling of wives, he says of Jesus, "He did not retaliate when He was insulted. When He suffered, He did not threaten to get even. He left his case in the hands of God, who always judges fairly," (1 Peter 2:23). A maturing wife learns how to leave her case in the hands of God, too. Even Jesus learned obedience through the things He suffered (Hebrews 5:8) and a wife grows more rapidly into Christ-likeness as she entrusts herself to Him. Jesus has the heart and understanding to identify with the unfairness a wife experiences. As she looks to and leans on Him, she will be sanctified. Her inner posture will say to her husband, "If you don't join me in this marriage I will be profoundly hurt, but I will not be crushed. I cannot pretend about my desire to share life with you in a rich way. I will never be free of that longing. However, I now refuse to be owned by it, because it is helping me taste Someone much bigger and kinder than you on a regular basis." This process is precious to God.

There is no believer, male or female, who can genuinely grow a restful heart without learning to endure through difficulty. Wives tend to think that their greatest problems in this world are external – a mean boss, a lack of financial security, or an uninvolved spouse. In truth, their greatest problems are the assaults of evil and the fleshly nature that they constantly fight. As they lean into their faith through relational tension and the way it connects them to Jesus, they will come to find rest in this world.

FEARLESSNESS

As a wife becomes more restful, she also becomes more of a revealing light in her husband's life. A deeper relationship with God gives her more clarity and confidence. She can more adequately see and name her husband's failures, and if she is less noisy, her husband will have a harder time dismissing her input. She will naturally trip over the moments where she can illuminate the darkness in her husband's heart, because she dislikes the space it will create between them. This is why a wife's call involves fearlessness – she can't be afraid to help her husband see his need for the Lord, even at the risk of disharmony in their marriage.

This is why Peter urges each woman to follow Sarah's example. He says, "You are her daughters when you do what is right without fear of what your husbands might do," (1 Peter 3:6). If you are at all familiar with Sarah's husband, Abraham, and his lack of character, you will appreciate what Peter is saying to wives. In the long Genesis narrative, Abraham responds well to God only twice: when he leaves Haran, and many years later when he takes Isaac up the mountain in obedience. In between, there is a span of more than 20 years when Abraham wrestles to believe and trust in God. Sarah lives in the wake of Abraham's growing and stumbling faith. In his fear and cowardice he lies, claiming Sarah as his sister. First, Pharaoh takes Sarah as his wife until the Lord supernaturally intervenes. Later, Abraham tells the same lie to Abimelech. He, too, takes Sarah as his wife until the Lord again intervenes.

The Old Testament does not detail the relationship between Abraham and Sarah other than to show that Abraham lied to protect himself and seemed willing to sacrifice Sarah at least twice. The narrative does not show us how Sarah related to Abraham in response to his unbelief. From Peter's comment, she must have continued to endure with Abraham and somehow she displayed courage and faith in the process. We know this because right after Peter counsels wives to act like Sarah, he recaps his overall advice on submission and says, "Now who is there to harm you if you are zealous for what is good? But even if you should suffer for righteousness sake, you will be blessed. Have no fear of them, nor be troubled, but in your hearts regard Christ the Lord as holy, always being prepared to make a defense to anyone who asks you for a reason for the hope that is in you; yet do it with gentleness and respect," (1 Peter 3:13-17, ESV).

Sarah must have helped Abraham grow in his faith with God. Perhaps the times Sarah endured with character helped facilitate moments that exposed Abraham's unbelief. So, when a wife patiently walks with her husband and allows God to work instead of forcing or manipulating change, she will find opportunities to become a megaphone that declares God is more necessary to her husband than he can conceive.

It would be nice if responding in a godly manner meant a wife would have a smoother relationship with her husband. In reality, her husband may become angry in an attempt to shelter his sin. I have seen this happen time and again. That's why Peter's advice seems important for every wife: "But even if you should suffer for righteousness sake, you will be blessed. Have no fear of them, nor be troubled, but in your hearts regard Christ the Lord as holy."

When a wife doesn't collude with her husband's sin, but exposes it by pursuing holiness, she ups the ante and risks her husband's anger or disapproval. Scripture often shows that humans don't respond well when their sins are revealed. Consider this Proverb, "Whoever rebukes a man will afterward find more favor than he who flatters with his tongue," (28:23, ESV). This implies that, at least initially, the uncovering of sin brings displeasure. It takes time for a guilty party to accept the reality of their sinfulness. So a wife is called to *fearlessness* as she awaits this period of acceptance.

Thus, when Peter wrote, "You are her daughters when you do what is right without fear of what your husbands might do," Peter is essentially saying, "Do not let your husband's misuse of his advantages cause you to shrink down with anxiety. Do not answer sin with sin during the time it takes him to really hear and trust God. Aim to respond well to your husband, but realize it may make your husband angrier. It will take deep faith to respond well, but it is the best way to help him cry out for God. At times you will help awaken your husband to things he needs to see and hear. Do not be afraid."

As her hope comes from God and her faith in the Lord's dealings with her husband, a wife can become restful and fearless at the same time. Such a wife is alive with the power and hope of the Gospel. She has left her case "in the hands of God, who always judges fairly," (1 Peter 2:23). Slowly and painstakingly she has turned over more and more of herself to Jesus. She is owned by His love and forgiveness. Her relationship with Jesus helps her grow an inner sense of buoyancy and power that she demonstrates in the way she lives. In some ways, she becomes a giant billboard that says to her husband, "This marriage is not about me! It can never be about me. It is about the One you spend too much time hiding from. Consider Him, run to Him, and cling to Him. Deal with Him. He is our hope."

12
STRENGTH

Wives, your longing to experience richness in relationships is a gift from God, but remember that like every gift in a fallen world, that longing easily can be misused. You know by now that your desire for connection will be frustrated, as evil wants you to step into a destructive role. There are many such roles, in fact. A wife may become demanding and nearly impossible to please. She may withdraw – physically, emotionally, or both. She may try to take care of her husband as if she were his mother. Evil loves to see a woman fall into these traps, because they keep her from pursuing her true calling to vulnerably work beside her husband to build Common Ground.

The strong, vulnerable wife declares to her husband, "My longing for richness in relationship is good. I cannot pretend about that. I will not beat you up with it, but I will not deny it as a way for you to get around your burden with futility. I won't turn my back on you. I will love and honor you so that you feel invited to stay in relationship with me." Solid feminine strength says, "God is in the future waiting to meet us with whatever we need to stand against evil and experience Common Ground. Don't shrink back. Walk with me toward it."

Evil is mightily threatened by feminine strength. In those moments where evil is working through her husband's sinfulness to oppress her, a wife needs strength simply to stand in the relationship and point her husband toward more. A virtuous woman is "clothed with *strength* and dignity, and she laughs with no fear of the future," (Proverbs 31:25). Feminine strength does not imply that a woman should take the marriage on her back, be strong enough to do her husband's part, or "buck up" and pretend she doesn't want something better. It is the strength to wait on the Lord and to believe He can do something she can't see, and to point her husband beyond his frustration with futility. It is the strength to stay alive to the hope of marital togetherness when she can't see it coming. Husbands, you need your wives to have this kind of strength.

STRENGTH TO EXPOSE

When a man and woman marry, she brings him face-to-face with the ways he has hidden and protected himself from his deep need for God. She is able to reveal his sin and expose his shortcomings in ways that no one else ever has. Since a woman has a longing for connection and a desire to share intimacy with her husband, she has spent most of her life dreaming of what marriage will be like. Then, somewhere in the first years of her marriage, she realizes that the reality doesn't match the fantasy. She may or may not realize that her mere presence often threatens her husband instead of drawing him to her, making him feel like an exposed criminal.

Before I got married, when I compared myself to other men I seemed humble, patient, and generous. Of course, none of my male friends spent too much time thinking about how I treated them and they didn't require that much from me. We could sit and watch a game, grunt a little, and have a great time.

When Dawn and I married and began sharing everything, it suddenly became clear that she wanted more from me than anybody I'd ever been close to. On the other side of making a lifetime commitment to each other, I began to get a sense of what that really meant. Now, if I wanted to go play basketball, I had to think about how it was going to impact Dawn. When we went out to dinner or spent time together after work, she wanted something out of that time that was different than what I wanted out of it. Slowly, I began to see that Dawn caused me to ask the question, "How much am I going to care about her?" I was faced with a dilemma. Do I lean into our marriage and aim to become a more involved husband or do I run for the hills? A lot of the time, I ran.

Once she realizes how she affects her husband, a wife usually tries to be less of a bother to him, or she tries to speed up the process and push him to "get it," instead of simply trusting that the exposure of marriage can lead him to brokenness, renewed faith, and greater intimacy over time. It isn't what she'd spent her girlhood dreaming of.

During our third year of marriage, I was working on my master's degree in Colorado. Dawn was working while I went to school. I had a natural base of friends at school, but it was a slower process for Dawn. She especially looked forward to spending extra time with me on the weekends.

Then two of my best friends, single guys, started planning a ski trip. I really wanted to go, but I was afraid to tell Dawn. I began to shut down around her because I figured she didn't want me to leave her for an entire weekend, when she was so lonely most of the time. But for weeks I kept talking up the trip, and dropping hints about it.

My wife is no dummy – she knew I'd been invited and wanted to go. She just let me keep talking. Finally, a few days before my friends were leaving, I mentioned the trip *again*. In a beautiful way Dawn said, "If you would like to go away skiing for the weekend, go, but please be man enough to let me be disappointed."

She did a masterful job exposing my weakness as a man. I tried to weasel my way into going on the trip by getting her to make the decision for me. She stayed alive, patiently waiting, and at a timely point let me see my fear. That weekend was terribly difficult for me, because I learned something painful. I never realized I disappointed people. I'd tried so hard my whole life to make others happy, and I thought I did – all the time. How unrealistic that was, and how blind I'd been. To choose to go away, knowing my wife was going to miss me and hurt being alone, made me face my people-pleasing nature in a big way. What a gift Dawn had given me.

> A wife moves along the path of redemption when she trusts what she sees without feeling the need to hammer it into her husband's consciousness.

Dawn began moving along the path of redemption when she trusted what she saw without feeling the need to hammer it into my consciousness. There'd been other times she'd made her case by strenuously citing a book, or a friend's opinion, or some other authority. More often than not I thought she didn't have confidence in her own beliefs and so I concluded, in my smug superiority, that they couldn't be valid. What I couldn't see was that my gifts threatened her and made her look for extra evidence to support her own viewpoint before she was willing to confront me. However, she also needed to go deeper with the Lord and hear His affirmation to be able to offer her wisdom with more confidence.

A wife's strength helps her keep faith when she becomes alert to her husband's blind spots. Often, what a husband really wants is quick affirmation that he's just great. However, as a wife gains the strength to let her husband experience the exposure of his weakness and sin, the more likely he is to receive an embrace from God. If a husband becomes instantly sanctified the minute he says, "I do," there's no need for him to have a wife who waits for him as he struggles through the sinful tendencies marriage makes so apparent. If, on the other hand, he has the tendency to use his gifts selfishly, then his wife needs to become alive in her feminine strength. She must let him endure through the exposure of his weaknesses and sins as a way to love him and fight against evil. In your marriage of Common Ground, you'll stand strong as you watch your husband be undone by marriage and then wait for God to set it right.

THE STRENGTH TO STAY OPEN

When a wife has looked forward to the connection marriage will bring her, it's hard to accept that she's not going to have a tension-free relationship with her husband on a regular basis anytime soon. I say it all the time: "God promises a lot up front; He just delivers slowly."

A marriage goes through a series of unending cycles of life and death. In a redemptive marriage, where the husband and wife are living out the Gospel together, there is often a period of death where the husband is really unnerved by the exposure the marriage brings. He usually become angrier and turns on his wife, trying to get her to stop exposing him. At this point, most women shut down in self-defense. They circle the wagons around themselves and their vulnerable hearts. Wives, that certainly seems to be a reasonable response, but this is the precise point where another facet of your strength can reveal itself if you'll allow it. Try to hold onto your desire for more, and simply wait, being willing to keep your heart open to this man you love.

For Dawn and me, this happened during the years our girls were being born. I was feeling the weight of adding children, a home, and a growing career to my plate and I selfishly thought Dawn should make all of that easier – not be an added source of difficulty. I became short with her, and more demanding. Dawn tried to help me see my sin in this, but I was too proud to listen. I punished her with distance as I threw myself into my work and my studies.

However, as we persevered, the Lord began to soften me and help me recognize my sin. I began to change, and started relating to Dawn with more openness and humility. Now she had to decide if she wanted to open up to me. It was the first time she had to choose this on a deep level. You see, once Dawn had experienced my cruelty over a span of time, it took much more faith for her to open up to me the way she'd been willing to do when we were first in love. The enemy taunted Dawn, saying, "Don't ever open up to Gordon again. He doesn't deserve it. Stay closed forever." Dawn now knew that our marriage was going to hurt in deep ways and she knew that the beautiful moments wouldn't last forever. Opening up at this new stage in marriage took significant strength.

It is very hard for a wife to walk through the pain marriage will bring her. The times Dawn has opened herself up to me after I've hurt her have transformed my heart more than any other human interaction. The author of the Song of Solomon grasped the very truth I'm trying to communicate. He wrote, "A garden locked is my sister, my bride, a spring locked, a fountain sealed," (Song of Solomon 4:12, ESV). In that day the four walls that surrounded a garden would act as a shield to protect it from predators. Only the owner of the garden could open the gate, and he would do so *from the inside*. In the same way, a wife holds the key to her heart.

Opening your heart always involves risk. God's burden demands that we drink deeply from His resources. Each wife has to grow the faith-filled strength necessary to open her heart to her husband. While he can grow into great maturity, no husband can guarantee his wife that he'll never hurt her again. No husband can pledge that the joyous times will last forever. No matter how mature a husband's love, a wife must still consciously decide to keep the gate to her heart open, despite the ache of past failure and the threat of future pain.

THE STRENGTH TO INVITE

A wife who regularly nurtures feelings of hurt, abandonment or rejection will almost always stop inviting her husband to share close moments. Her pain may be so deep, or may have lasted so long, that she may have forgotten how. She may feel so defeated by her burden that she's tried to deaden her longing for relationship. God asks a further degree of endurance from her – the strength to keep inviting her husband into relationship.

This type of strength or endurance can easily be confused with being a doormat or an enabler. It takes discernment to know the difference. The type of strength I'm talking about happens as a wife grows a redemptive love that longs to be part of restoration. As Jesus increases in a wife, she becomes more like Him. She will not stand for abuse, but she is patient through trial. She refuses the temptation to become cold or unavailable. Thus, with her life, she learns to say to her husband, "I will not deaden my femininity to make your calling less toilsome. Instead, I will keep inviting you to care for me, because as you learn to endure through futility and strengthen our relationship, it will help us grow together and help you grow into a man in every other area of your life." Through the marital relationship a husband engages evil directly by learning to be more understanding and sacrificial toward his wife. A wife can help persuade him into more by not letting go of a longing to be known and enjoyed. As a wife does this and a husband responds, he will grow spiritual strength to fight through evil. (I regularly see the other extreme, where husbands slowly pull away from their wives and cave in to the shaming, accusatory voice of evil telling them to give up. This defeat in marriage pushes a man toward cowardice in all the other areas of his life as well.)

The hard part for a wife is that this means encouraging her husband through his weaknesses. Essentially, a wife is saying to her husband, "Don't give up your desire to love me well and enjoy me. This quest is too necessary for our marriage and for your growth as a man. It hurts me and it hurts you that you can't get it right, but as you endure, God will surprise us with Common Ground." When a wife displays this courageous kind of love, it is the opposite of reflexive self-protection. I call it painful self-abandonment. The wife becomes willing to say, "I will not close off my heart and my longings because you make mistakes. I want more for you and for me. This will keep pointing us to Jesus and our need for His sustaining love. As we find more of Him, you will grow endurance and I will grow vibrancy. This is too necessary for our faith."

STRONG AND STEADFAST

A wife's longing for connection and her desire to be enjoyed by the man in her life is a reflection of the feminine heart of God. Despite our nearly constant rejection, God continues to bid us – His beloved ones – to come to Him. Likewise, a wife will inevitably face rejection by her husband. But in the face of that pain she can come alive to

God's heart and strength, which dwell within and through her. She will grow the strength to issue yet another gentle invitation to her husband, beckoning him toward a more refreshing marriage.

Like God, a wife must learn to do this in the face of loss. God's children regularly turn from Him. We miss rich opportunities to experience His great love. A husband will miss opportunities to enjoy his wife's beauty, which can never be recovered. A wife can learn to grieve this, let Jesus hold her, and yet continue inviting her husband to her so that they can grow into more over time. Such future enjoyment has the potential to be even more meaningful because it comes despite past loss. This is why moments of Common Ground are so profound – they mock past failure.

When we met, I was initially fascinated with Dawn because she was attractive and had an engaging personality. When we were dating, there were times that her laughter, passion, and freedom overwhelmed me with a sense of beauty far more irresistible than her physical beauty. I am sad as I write this – so many times I use my gifts to smother that fire inside her. I sorrow over the fact that she fearfully took me as seriously as I took myself. I am so, so sorry that she wasn't able to laugh at me more, and I grieve the loss of all the laughter we might have shared together. In many ways, her calling in those long years of our marriage was to help me see my poverty in the Gospel.

When a wife grows the strength to stay alive in marriage, she helps her husband to resist evil. Evil will continually tell him he doesn't have what it takes to go the long haul with his wife. In the moments when a wife is at rest but her husband is afraid, she helps him to see and hear God. When she is present enough to open up to her husband even though he's hurt her, she makes the Gospel real for him. As a wife keeps inviting her husband toward her, she reminds him that he has something much better alive in him than he remembers – the life of Christ. A husband needs help to submit to

God and resist evil. In the instances where a wife lives with strength, she becomes a life-giving picture of the Gospel.

13

WINSOMENESS

A winsome woman is not a silly woman, nor is she a frivolous one. A winsome woman sees beyond the moment. Not only does she rest in the Lord's goodness, but she is able to believe the best about her husband, even when he messes up – again. She's willing to laugh *with* him, not *at* him, and she's also able to laugh at herself. She trusts the Lord well enough that she can release her fear of future doom. She refuses to believe evil's lies that her husband doesn't care about her, just because he makes mistakes. She is willing to examine her own heart, and lovingly admit her own faults and failings. She radiates peace and contentment.

The wise man in Proverbs describes a virtuous woman: "She is clothed with strength and dignity and *she laughs with no fear of the future,*" (Proverbs 31:25). I call that winsome. A winsome woman walks in grace with her husband, because she is not owned by fear of what may come.

It's not easy for her to do. Think of her in the same context as the Israelites wandering the desert. After 40 years, the Lord essentially said to them, "Listen, guys, I don't get it. You had food every day and your sandals never wore out. I don't understand why everything was so hard," (Deuteronomy 29:5). I think they would have answered, "Lord, we didn't know where we were going, and we were not sure if You would get us there." The Israelites' day-to-day experiences would have been so much more restful (and encouraging to one another) if they had trusted more in what God had promised. Their daily needs were met, but they listened to, focused on, and agreed with lies from the evil one. That was what kept them from daily rest.

> A winsome woman trusts the Lord well enough that she can release her fear of future doom.

A wife often interprets life through the same kind of lens, one that's clouded by potential doom. She wants her husband's performance to guarantee her a pain-free future, but it can't. By aiming for winsomeness, she gains rest in the moment. It also helps her keep her husband's performance in proper perspective. When she has more faith to resist the way evil wants her to misread her husband's daily imperfections, she can remember he is only human.

Winsomeness, a mixture of mercy and laughter, helps her to keep cooperating with her husband in the present while also looking toward more in the future. As she is able to genuinely recognize her sin – and believe that she is as much of a sinner as her husband – she will have some mercy to give him. Once she gets to know Jesus through deeper repentance, she begins to believe that He can redeem any moment and that He is big enough to work all things together for good.

RELATIONSHIP-RIGHTEOUSNESS

A wife can't be winsome when she stands in judgment of her husband's failures. When that happens, she feels justified in not cooperating with her husband to work against evil. She becomes smug and acts morally superior, because she believes her virtue has grown out of her own effort. The Scriptures condemn self-righteousness – if you form genuine biblical character, it comes as a gift from God. No man or woman becomes a better person apart from the grace and mercy of God. It is not something you earn.

Evil plays on the gender differences between men and women to incite what I call relationship-righteousness. A wife's longing for connection often causes her to do more to make the marriage work. Because her busy-ness has good intentions, she may believe the lie that her husband's passivity means he does not care for her or for the quality of their relationship. In addition, because a wife usually brings more relational experience into marriage, evil has no problem convincing her that she's the expert. Evil plays on the created differences between men and women to keep a wife focused on her husband's mistakes so that she judges him as being relationally inferior.

But evil began his work in her even before she married. Because of the vulnerability women face in this world, most women bring gender-based resentments into marriage. Fathers, brothers, classmates, friends, and boyfriends may have taken advantage of her, or just as damaging, been indifferent to her. Almost all women have experienced inappropriate comments, touches, relational roughness or indifference by men in their lives, and sometimes from the men closest to them. Far more than men, women grow up having experienced, internalized, and attached themselves to such wounds in a concentrated way. There is often an unfelt sorrow that grows into resentment. Larry Crabb notes, "Women have learned to be skeptical. Every little girl has discovered that not everything wonderful about her will be reliably enjoyed. Some of who she is will at times be ignored, despised, demeaned, or selfishly used. In a fallen world, she learns that offering all that she is to another runs the terrible risk of rejection and abuse. And because she too is fallen and therefore committed to her own well-being with no thought of dependence of God, she figures out how to minimize the risks by hiding the tenderest parts of her soul and avoiding an honest look at her ugly parts."

Minimizing the "tenderest parts of her heart and avoiding an honest look at her ugly parts" is how a woman buckles under the assaults of evil, developing a fleshly hostility toward men that becomes relationship-righteousness. Any wounding a young girl experiences almost always intensifies through her life as she learns to self-protectively balance the assaults of rejection and harm from men with effort, manipulation, or control to gain an illusion of safety or connection that is soothing. When a girl reflexively self-protects and grows into adulthood without significant softening, her fleshly nature will be intensified with hostility toward men.

When a woman chooses her own ways to soothe the ache of living in this sinful world, while refusing to be humbled and redeemed by her burden, she will feel proud. This fleshly hardness in her is actually enmity toward God. Her flesh is hostile toward God and it has pulled her toward rebuffing her need for Him. *Her flesh will be most aroused when she is confronted with her need to be more vulnerable and her lack of vulnerability will always show up most clearly in relationship with her husband.* The majority of women show up in marriage with relationship-righteousness. It may – and often does – take time to show itself in the marriage, but it almost always will.

It is so easy for evil to inflame this. Because a wife wants more out of relationship, it is easy for her to have a vast supply of her husband's failures ready as ammunition if needed. It is easy for most women to outwit a man in a discussion about relational behavior. However, her insight into relationship is a gift – it grows out of God's design. She doesn't see these things because she is better; she sees them because she is more vulnerable. *Her quest should be to learn to use what she sees redemptively and not punitively.* A wife's resentment, fear of the future, and insight into her husband's life all work together to help her stand in judgment over her husband. This pleases evil, who wants a wife hardening toward her husband. Evil's message? That the husband is too dangerous or too inept to be trusted. And evil likes it even better when the wife delivers that message.

The created differences between men and women were meant to provide a richness and beauty to life. Evil wants an arrogant hardness to exist between men and women and he wants that hardness to be provoked by God's created differences. He wants a wife to hate her vulnerability and he wants a husband to detest a call toward patient involvement. *Thus, evil loves when a man uses his advantages to take what he wants from a woman. He also loves when a wife uses her relational deftness to emasculate her husband.* A woman who resents God's design and the relational disappointment it brings her in life will attach herself to the failures of the man in her world and camp on them. To one degree or another, each wife will have some form of relationship-righteousness that pulls her toward emasculating her husband. It is not just a hardness to protect herself, it is an evil-inspired hardness meant to prove that God was wrong when he created men and women differently.

RELATIONSHIP-RIGHTEOUSNESS: HOW EVIL USES IT AGAINST HUSBANDS

In general, a wife internalizes the problems in the relationship long before a man does. Husbands often need help defining the depth of the marital problems. However, this does not mean that she sees everything with perfect clarity or can come up with a solution to the problem on her own. The fact that she is impacted by the problem sooner than her husband leads to this relationship-righteousness. Wives often devise solutions that are heavily weighted on masculine repentance and are too quick and/or too heavy-handed. Evil regularly takes advantage of what a wife sees and heightens the problem by planting those kinds of solutions in her mind.

With most couples, the wife will see the marriage as far worse than it is. Commonly, she'll come up with a long list of what they must do to fix their problems, and often has it written up or can recite it at request. She is ready to get busy and make things better. She avoids a call to faith, instead letting herself be pulled toward working out their problems through effort. Foolishly, she thinks her husband is the whole problem, and she lets him know it, even though it reinforces his passivity. You see, he thinks they're going to play catch, so he gets out his glove as they step out into the yard. Then his wife launches 100 baseballs at him in 20 seconds, and he throws his hands over his head and curls up into a ball.

In those moments, I want both the husband and wife to sorrow together about how they have sinned. Many times, the wife is too afraid to do this because she feels that by making such an admission, she is throwing away control. Holding onto her husband's failures has given her a sense of power. It is not a very redemptive sense of power or even a helpful one, but when she feels vulnerable, she reaches out for whatever will give her the quickest sense of support. In subtle, unseen ways, a wife becomes attached to using marital guilt. It often gets a husband (especially a Christian one) going and it seems like redemption.

I believe Timothy is addressing what I am calling relationship-righteousness when he writes, "Women should listen and learn quietly and submissively. I do not let women teach men or have authority over them. Let them listen quietly. For God made Adam first, and afterward he made Eve. And it was the woman, not Adam, who was deceived by Satan, and sin was the result," (1 Timothy 2:11-14). I would encourage wives to hear it this way: "Wives, in the flesh you will hate your vulnerability and will love to hold things over your husband. You will see your husbands' sin very clearly and will want to correct them. You forget that evil will take what you see and twist it. This is why he often tries to deceive you into relationship-righteousness as a way to divide you and your spouse. The Lord has fashioned husbands in a way that you need them. Give yourself and your insight vulnerably to him and help to call forth his ability to remember the Gospel over time. As you wait for him in the process, you will become closer to the Lord and more secure in His love. Your ability to see into your husband is a gift God has given you. Use that gift wisely."

SELF-RIGHTEOUSNESS: HOW TO TURN FROM IT

The quickest way for a wife to disarm self-righteousness is to become aware of the way she nurtures injustice. Evil wants a wife to remain angry because God asks her to be vulnerable. A person who is more vulnerable in a relationship can have a tendency to dwell on the ways he or she is treated unfairly. A wife needs help to intentionally keep remembering and replaying her mental videotape of her husband's failures. She must look for and cultivate the places and relationships that Jesus will use to help her turn from relationship-righteousness. A good relationship for a wife is not one where she gets together with friends to chew over their husbands' failures. It is one where her friends help her see both what is redemptive and sinful about her and her husband, and encourage her to move toward more.

Evil often pulls a wife to focus so much on her husband's sin that she can't see hers in comparison. She keeps running to Jesus to get His help for her feelings of marital rejection, but rarely seeks His forgiveness for her own marital sin. The parable of the unforgiving debtor (Matthew 18:21-35) is instructive on this matter. In this parable, a man is freed from a great debt he owes the king, but then refuses to forgive a lesser debt owed him by a fellow servant. The king calls in the forgiven man and says, "You evil servant! I forgave you that tremendous debt because you pleaded with me. Shouldn't you have mercy on your fellow servant, just as I had mercy on you?" (Matthew 18:32-33).

If a wife wants to turn from treating her husband with relationship-righteousness, she must come to appreciate that Jesus has forgiven her far more than she has forgiven her husband. She will not move toward this because she sees the need to do it. She must learn to hear and believe a revealed truth that confronts her marital self-righteousness. A wife will have to learn to tell herself (and she will need to hear from her friends) that she is as much a sinner as her husband. She will have to plead with the Lord to make the parable of the unforgiving debtor real to her. A wife's posture of relationship-righteousness has only one place to find a home. It must be nailed right to the cross where Jesus died for her sins.

If a wife walks through that process, she will grow winsomeness. Tasting His goodness helps her release the hold her husband's sins and brokenness have on her. They no longer own her in the same way, and she will begin to laugh a little more at the future. Her laughter, in light of her husband's failures, says, "I am not unnerved by your sin. It is just like mine, and you can find more of Jesus just like I do. He is helping me to wait for you and I believe that He will redeem the wounds I receive from you."

A wife doesn't learn to laugh without fear of the future by pretending about life or by getting her husband to perform better. She learns to laugh when she receives deep forgiveness from God. She will see how she has worked against the thing she wants most – a rich relationship with her husband – by sinning against her husband. When she can hear Jesus say, "That's OK. You weren't supposed to be able to earn it. I died so I could give it to you as a gift," she is on her way to laughter. Jesus is the One who leads us through the darkness and as a wife really gets to know Him, she learns how to laugh at evil and his oppressive ways.

MARTYRDOM BLOCKS REPENTANCE

If a wife confronts her relationship-righteousness and softens, she will grow a mercy and laughter that helps her husband endure in his calling. Evil tries to block a wife's call to winsomeness by pushing her toward becoming a martyr. A wife will fall into martyrdom if she tries to grow mercy before strength. Because a husband is so apt to use his advantages selfishly, a wife must first learn to walk the pathway of strength and invite her husband to deal meaningfully with his masculine indifference before she grows the mercy to help him endure.

It was hard for Dawn to grow out of martyrdom. She often let me bully her when I was wrong. I wish she had been more able to look at me with hopeful laughter and say, "Let's go to the movies." I would have been upset and accused her of not really caring about me, our marriage, or the truth. The heart of a great response would have been for her to say, "Gordon, the more I try to be what you want, the more I move away from being what you need. We can work really hard tonight to solve our problems or we can go to the movies, hold hands, and taste in a small way that we are still for each other. You judge me unjustly when you think I don't love the truth because I don't say as much as you or read books as much as you. Sometimes your activity is a cover for your fear and insecurity. Come laugh with me, my friend, and help me welcome the Kingdom of God that is advancing into our midst."

Instead, what Dawn found herself saying was, "I keep trying harder to do what you want me to and still you are not happy." She was sacrificing, trying to be someone and something she wasn't, and becoming more resentful every day. For a while this kept her away from repentance and from seeing her proclivity toward martyrdom. She got busy trying to solve things instead of listening to the Lord. He was saying to her, "Stop sacrificing so much. Stop being a martyr. Stop doing what Gordon thinks you should do when he is afraid and nervous. I don't want your sacrifices. I want your allegiance. Laugh with Me some. I have already died for the sin you and Gordon are struggling with, and I will overcome it. I want you to trust Me to live through you in the midst of rejection. I brought you together so you could unnerve Gordon's pride. Don't turn away from your fun-loving nature. Just let Me stand up inside of you in the face of rejection. Stop trying to buy Me and Gordon off with your sacrifices."

For a wife to begin turning away from relationship-righteousness, the couple must have advanced much farther into the enemy's camp. The husband's humility and openness and the wife's strength create a platform that helps a wife step into winsomeness. As she more easily recognizes her resentment, fear of the future, and propensity to be a martyr, she will grow in winsomeness. Dawn, like every wife, wanted to buy God off with sacrifices instead of walking in submission to His purposes. Evil will use a husband's advantages and a wife's vulnerability to push her away from awe-inspired cooperation and restful fearlessness. Relationship-righteousness will be one large obstacle in this path. As she goes deeper and turns from relationship-righteousness, she can find winsomeness that helps her laugh without fear of the future. She can learn to stand in grace with her husband because she knows he doesn't hold the key to future Common Ground.

14

OTHER-CENTERED ENCOURAGEMENT

Walking the pathways of strength and winsomeness are high callings for a wife, but other-centered encouragement is the highest. Evil will always try to get a wife's involvement with her husband to be about herself and what she needs. He will make it profoundly difficult for a wife to encourage her husband for his own sake. Because of evil's influence, a wife is great at encouraging her spouse to be a better husband or father. When he succeeds, she gets something in return. The hardest thing for a wife to do is to encourage her husband through difficulty whether or not it has a direct impact on her or the family.

Any wife that has grown the strength to stand up to relational pain and the mercy to turn away from relationship-righteousness is ready to grow into this part of her calling. She is prepared to step into the darkness that assails her husband and encourage him toward more, whether or not she directly benefits from her sacrifice.

A wife's third pathway is a much fuller form of love and penetrates much deeper into the evil one's territory. This is because a wife steps out of herself more fully and communicates to her husband that his life is about more than her. The first two pathways are more directly related to helping a husband deal with his discomfort in marriage and his need to grow as a husband; the third is pointed at helping a husband for his own sake. When a wife grows into other-centered encouragement, she shows the deepest form of marital love.

NOURISHING A LITTLE INTO MORE

A wife is called to recognize where Christ is alive in her husband and affirm that – however small it might seem to her. It will often feel foolish to a wife to encourage her husband's growth when it seems so small compared to what she wants. When she submits to God's call to appreciate her husband, and resists evil's pull to tear him down, she will be free to give other-centered encouragement as a gift.

To grow into good other-centered encouragement, a wife must remember how the Kingdom of God grows in every person's heart. As he taught, Jesus addressed the nature of Kingdom growth. He said that the Kingdom of God grows like a tiny mustard seed into a tree or like a bit of yeast, which starts small and permeates every part of the dough (Luke 13:18-21).

Christ offered these parables as an attempt to help the Pharisees understand their misguided notions about how growth should occur. Like the Pharisees, we all want Kingdom growth to happen quickly when it reinforces our own selfish desires. A husband's gradual growth is always a reminder to a wife that God works slowly. It keeps her seeing and depending on her relationship with the Lord, and not on her husband, for buoyancy. To encourage her husband wherever he is in his process of growth, a wife must resist the evil-inspired pull to get him busy on all the other improvements she sees he could make. She needs to remember that the Kingdom of God in her husband's heart will grow slowly.

THE PAIN OF ALONENESS

In most marriages, I have watched wives become preoccupied with their needs because they face pain they were not prepared for. Most women entered their marriages presuming their struggle with loneliness would end. When it doesn't, they're acutely distressed.

The book of Proverbs confirms the aloneness we must face as humans. It says, "Each heart knows its own bitterness, and no one else can fully share its joy," (Proverbs 14:10). The wise man was saying, "There is a level of loneliness in this world that no one can take away." As a wife bumps up against profound loneliness, even when she's secure in her husband's love, she has an opportunity to reach out for Jesus. It may happen when her husband is zoned out watching TV on their honeymoon, or when he's away on a business trip, or when she is home with young children crawling along the floor, or when she sits in her youngest child's room after dropping him off at college. To a wife, however, these periods of loneliness can seem like a grand betrayal. Those moments will feel like death. Not death of something that she needed to live, but death of an illusion – that her loneliness would be cured this side of heaven.

Many wives have a deep desire to "solve" the ache of loneliness on their own. Instead, they must learn to wait in loneliness if they want to be a blessing to their husbands. Reflecting on this, Sharon Hersch writes, "When a woman courageously stares into the eyes of her desperation, she need not collapse in shame or cover up with pretense. The yearning for relationship is not an indication that something is wrong with her, but that something is profoundly right.

... Extravagant love is lonely. I used to believe that maturity was the absence of this angst I seem to have been born with. I am learning that maturity is not the absence of longing, but it is the ability to wait in loneliness."

When a woman waits in loneliness, instead of solving her pain by her own methods, she is praying that God would nourish the life of Christ in her. Paul says, "I pray that from His glorious, unlimited resources, He will give you mighty inner strength through His Holy Spirit. And I pray that Christ will be more and more at home in your hearts as you trust in Him. May your roots go down deep into the soil of God's marvelous love," (Ephesians 3:16-17). As a wife waits in loneliness, her roots are going down deep into the soil of God's marvelous love. The nourishment she finds in periods of aloneness will lead to richer relationships, because as a woman waits for God in aloneness, she will be formed into Christ's image. He is a pursuing, reconciling God. If a wife wants to have a richer relational world and does not want the burden of relational

> Marriage does not carry nearly enough meaning to bring rest to a wife's heart.

pain to own her, then she must learn to wait in loneliness so that more of Christ is formed in her and she has a newfound freedom to pursue others through pain and darkness.

Over time, if she endures, she will embrace the paradox of the Gospel. She will look back and realize that the life of Christ was growing inside of her during lonely periods, which actually freed her to love more richly. It is through those moments where, like the Psalmist, a wife learns this refrain: "Whom have I in heaven but you? I desire you more than anything on earth. My health may fail, and my spirit may grow weak, but God remains the strength of my heart; He is mine forever," (Psalm 73:25-26).

LIVING INSIDE AND OUTSIDE THE MARRIAGE

Waiting in loneliness helps a wife to silence self-absorption and nourish Christ in her heart, which in turn gives her spiritual sustenance to be more of an encouragement to her husband. She must also begin to feel more comfortable living outside her marriage. With the presence of a man in her life, a wife often forgets that she is made for more than just togetherness with him. As humans, we love to make idols. If we find something that promises to bring us life, we will make it an idol. This is what a wife often does with her husband and marriage. As a means of grace to help you deal with the idolatry that can go along with marriage, the Lord wants you to find meaning outside your relationship with your husband. A wife's dominant passions occur within the sphere of close relationship, but she's unwise to expend all her energies there. As a wife cultivates that part of her that longs to have impact in this world, and as she loosens her grip on the part of her that craves connection, she is growing a deeper character.

In some ways the "stay-at-home mom" model has worked against wives seeking to grow true biblical character. A woman who, because of fear, chooses to stay within the four walls of her home and does not engage meaningfully with the world is missing the mark. By the same token, so is a man who spends all his waking hours outside of the home. The Gospel is always about more. For the majority of human history, family and home have been a shared venture. In an agrarian culture, the family lived and worked together. When the children were not being schooled, they were out in the fields with their dad (and often their mom) as soon as they were old enough to help.

Today's role as a stay-at-home-mother is more a result of the industrial revolution than it is a reflection of biblical wisdom.

"She goes out to inspect a field and buys it; with her earnings she plants a vineyard. She extends a helping hand to the poor and opens her arms to the needy," (Proverbs 31:16, 20). The wife described in Proverbs 31 engages in commerce without her husband. She was out in the world engaged in business and was advancing God's kingdom. In the Old Testament, there is really no larger demonstration of faith than caring for the poor and needy. The wife was about more than caring for her family. Living outside of the family was part of her everyday life.

As a wife begins to put focus and energy outside of her marriage and family, two things happen at once:

- She finds meaning in her efforts.
- She must exercise increased faith to be involved in the world.

We are meaning-seeking creatures. Marriage does not carry nearly enough meaning to bring rest to a wife's heart. As a wife finds life outside her marriage, the marital relationship becomes lighter to both her husband and herself. In addition, there is a different element of mystery and struggle involved in the world outside the home. The teaching of the New Testament clearly demonstrates that along the path of sanctification, difficulty is one of our greatest gifts. As a wife encounters obstacles and challenges outside the home, she is presented with opportunities to walk in faith and to grow. For many wives, home can be a place to hide.

If a wife is aiming to embody the character of Christ, she must begin to recognize that her marriage and her husband are only a part of that process. Her marital relationship and the involvement of her husband ought to provide a taste of the Gospel, but it cannot be the only table she eats from. Meaningful engagement outside the home helps a wife to experience opportunities to live out the Gospel and taste life while also allowing her to bump up against difficulties that will help her grow in faith. This, too, will help alleviate the ache of aloneness and help her step out of self-absorption.

HONORING TRUE BEAUTY

In addition to succumbing to the pain of aloneness and hiding within the home, a wife's self-absorption is also aggravated by cooperating with evil's perversion of beauty. From the time the New Testament was written until now, women have believed the lie that their outward beauty is a source of power, that it motivates men, and that it can reduce their loneliness and inner angst. This will never be true. Make no mistake – feeling attractive is an essential part of a woman, and there's not a thing wrong with wearing pretty clothes and paying attention to your appearance. But you cannot solve your loneliness primarily by enhancing your outer beauty.

Unfortunately, men play right into this lie as well. The rampant use of pornography is an indicator of how much men worship false beauty. An airbrushed photograph can never represent true beauty, however perfect the woman may appear. A husband and wife's lustful flight toward counterfeit beauty keeps a wife focused on herself. Every woman falls short of physical perfection. This will never change. If a wife tries to achieve physical perfection, or if her husband pressures her to do so, they are reinforcing her self-absorption. When husbands and wives cooperate with Satan's view of beauty – like outward perfection – it breeds idolatry. This actually increases a women's sense of shame and subsequent self-absorption. As wives keep trying to be something they can't be, and as husbands affirm this, a mocking cloud of shame will push on a wife and diminish her presence. Instead of finding true beauty, she and her husband find only emptiness and distance.

Humans want to experience beauty without brokenness and sacrifice. Physical imperfections can humble you and increase your hunger and need for God, which will lead to more Common Ground. This is the only way you can experience true beauty on this side of heaven and it requires patience, forgiveness, and endurance. A marriage should help a wife grow into a sense that both her physical body and her whole person are gifts that helps her husband find rest.

The woman in the Song of Solomon portrays a biblical example of this concept as she bids her man toward her without reservation. "Awake, north wind! Come, south wind! Blow on my garden and waft its lovely perfume to my lover. Let him come into his garden and eat its choicest fruits," (Song of Solomon 4:16). Unfortunately, few Christian wives would feel this beautiful and confident in inviting their husbands toward them.

If you read through Song of Solomon, you will see the woman represented in this passage believes there is something about her that the man will enjoy inside and outside the bedroom. The alluring, sensual interplay between the man and the women is not just about lovemaking. The sexual overtones of this Old Testament book are a picture of the entirety of the relationship between the man and the woman. It is complete, full, beautiful Common Ground.

A GIFT THAT PIERCES DARKNESS

Waiting in loneliness nourishes and strengthens the inner part of a wife. Finding meaning and life outside the marriage refreshes the wife. Embracing true beauty in a marriage calls more of her inner beauty out into the relationship. Each of those areas help the wife to move through self-absorption so that she sees her husband better and has more to give him. Sometimes, that encouragement may be only a single sentence, but it's the sentence he needs.

One morning, Dawn asked me what my day was going to be like. I talked a little about some of the difficulties I expected to face, and she looked thoughtful before she replied. "You sure have to fight a lot of battles." Nine words. It may seem like a throwaway line to you, but it wasn't to me. You see, I'd gotten used to how much Dawn resented my work and the toll it took on me, because it meant she got less of me. It seemed like any time I mentioned one of my problems or troubles, we got into the "who has the harder life" argument. That morning, when she replied with genuine warmth, her words surrounded me. She saw the part of me that wants to battle well but is often tired or resentful and she called it to life. *It was a simple comment, but it owned me the rest of the day.* Her spirit spoke to my spirit and I was encouraged to battle evil with more resolve. That morning she stepped over her needs, along with any resentment or fear that she felt, and surrounded me with warmth simply by acknowledging my difficulties. I felt her femininity surrounding me and touching the inner part of my heart.

> A wife battles evil most profoundly when she steps into her husband's world and offers encouragement that is just for him.

Because evil will look for vulnerable times to attack a couple, a wife must also grow the wisdom to come alive to moments when she needs to encourage her husband in an even deeper way, which will reach into his soul and help him to resist evil more powerfully.

I will never forget the first time I experienced this from Dawn. I was in the midst of a job search that had been 12 years in the making.

I felt called to ministry as a sophomore in college, but the Lord led me on a winding path before I was ready to pursue the call full-time. Finally, I was prepared to live the dream – but the job search went on for months. The longer it dragged on, the more dejected and withdrawn I became. Eight months earlier, Dawn had given birth to our first child, Aimee. Having a baby added extra pressure to the search and caused me to question even more whether I could find employment that would provide for a growing family. It seemed like my dream was dying, and my despair filled our marriage. As the search dragged on, our relationship became more conflicted.

At the end of one day I came home and Dawn, Aimee, and I sat down on the couch. The card Dawn handed said: "Blessed are those who have not seen and yet have believed." Dawn signed the card as if Aimee had written the message. It said, "Daddy, Mom and I believe in you. We know you'll go good places and do good things. You have taken very good care of us. Thank you. This is a reminder of all the good things inside of you and all the great things you'll do in the future. We love you."

After I read the card, I opened a present from them. It was a book – *Oh, the Places You'll Go!* by Dr. Seuss. I was so moved as I read through the book and talked with Dawn about my dreams. Though she was often lost in the challenges and joys of becoming a new mother, her card and gift demonstrated how much she was still aware of what I might need in my time of struggle. I was in a funk and it was no fun to be around me, but Dawn stepped out of her world, looked at life from my perspective, and spoke deeply into my heart.

She could easily have scolded me for being neglectful or reminded me how much the family was counting on me, and she would have been right. I was despairing and angry and Dawn had to fight through fear and resentment to step into the darkness around me. As I read the card and the book, with its sweet, simple, cheerful message, her presence pierced the hardness in my heart and nourished my faith.

One reason it softened me was that her gift was an extension of her presence. She was being unselfish, but she was still being herself. I'd thought I needed Dawn to me help with my resume or track down more job contacts. But she gave me a children's book that took me outside my fleshly way of approaching life. Through her gift she said, "I am here with you to help you understand that true worship means we can laugh in the midst of evil's oppressive onslaught." Dawn is most feminine and most herself when she calls me to laugh as a way to worship and to say with her that God is in control. In that moment she surrounded me with her beauty and stood in the gap by stepping over her fear of how I might respond and courageously encouraging me.

When a wife has the maturity to agree with the Spirit, she can move into the husband's world and encourage him, instead of leaving him to fight alone. The Spirit will use her actions to penetrate her husband's hardness and he will be invited to stand up and resist the evil that tries to overpower him.

As a wife walks the pathway of other-centered encouragement, she demonstrates her hatred of evil and the way it tries to oppress her husband. She grows the dignity of loving well. A wife, just like a husband, is called to battle evil. You do this most profoundly when you step into your husband's world as darkness assaults him and help him resist evil by offering encouragement that is just for him.

15

ALMOST HEAVEN

For many, many years I had no idea Dawn and I would discover togetherness that is both restful and nourishing, because our relationship was so often awkward, difficult and draining. In my head I believed God works all things together for good, but as our marriage evolved, it didn't seem as if He would do that for us in this lifetime. I began to conclude that when it came to marriage, "all things working together for good" must take place only in heaven. Heaven – a believer's eternal home of rest and beauty, where the very language you will speak is love. Evil will be destroyed and Christ will take his rightful throne as king. There will be no more tears (Revelation 7:17), swords will be turned into plowshares (Isaiah 2:4), and you will rest in God's full knowledge of you (1 Corinthians 13:12).

It now seems ironic that I have a sense of what heaven is like because I have tasted it in my marriage. There was a time when I depended on the promise of heaven to help me endure in marriage. *Now I look forward to heaven and see it coming because I am watching it unfold in my marriage.* Because the Lord has helped us work together to disarm evil, Dawn and I experience more tastes of heaven. As we turned from the flesh, submitted to God and resisted evil by walking pathways of redemption, we share Common Ground. As we journeyed up the mountain the way God called us, and kept listening to His guidance, we went higher and higher despite the challenges and frustrations along the way. We are now surrounded by more beauty on a regular basis than when we first started our climb. We have maturity to stand against divisiveness, the tension between us does not grow as hastily as it once did and we are quicker to be kind to one another. We feel known and embraced in a way that can be similar to being fully known by the Lord. Evil is not as free to harass us or divide us. More and more, our journey up the mountain of marriage now seems like we are traveling home to the place where we belong. Lord willing, we have miles left to travel together and more beauty to experience, but we are grateful for how different the atmosphere around us has become.

During the years we were living so recklessly in the flesh and learning to walk our redemptive pathways, we regularly missed the mark when it came to working together. Because of the ongoing warfare, we needed faith to stay at marriage. Although there were many times I wanted to turn away from Dawn, and many times I did, *every time I ran into the Lord He encouraged me back toward her.*

CELEBRATING THE FRUIT OF THE PROCESS

As you come to understand that marriage involves warfare that blinds you, you will increasingly need to trust the Lord and His process of moving forward. As that way of walking in marriage becomes more natural to you, it becomes infinitely more important to celebrate the small victories you experience along the way, because a marriage of Common Ground will be filled with both heartache and beauty.

There will be moments where the beauty of redemption seems very small compared to the disappointment. The enemy loves to rob and kill and destroy, and you understand now that at times you will participate with him against your marriage. In my marriage, we've marred potentially wonderful good moments – like a dinner out, or a weekend getaway – by our selfishness. We can't get those moments back. When a couple can sorrow together through the selfishness and loss that enter their marriage, they are experiencing rich moments of Common Ground. It's an important way to keep moving forward.

Marriage can never be one constant state of Common Ground. The ongoing wounding you experience, even as you are sanctified, serves as a reminder that you live in a fallen world dependent on God's continual graciousness. Thus, a large part of the motivation to continue on in marriage grows out of celebrating redemption in the midst of a fallen world. Moments of Common Ground bring hope that you are moving toward a time when you will one day live in a world defined by it.

In a redemptive marriage, the life-giving moments of beauty start small and grow over time until you begin to trust they will keep coming. The intensity with which evil attacks marriage – and the difficulties that result – make it important to celebrate any good changes God brings into your marriage.

I remember when I began to realize how immature I was in the area of hope. I still wanted perfection and I know I felt that one bad thing outweighed all the good. As I realized more deeply how much evil works against what is good and holy, I started being more moved and surprised when we experienced redemption. I began to think, "One true moment, one honorable act, and one right, pure, lovely, or admirable response is excellent and worthy of praise," (Philippians

4:8). I began to attach myself to these hopeful moments intentionally, even when it seemed foolish. Those moments made clear that God was working for our marriage, and our celebration turned into worship.

Each couple I've worked with has experienced both beauty and disappointment in their marriage. However, the couples that have the hardest time finding Common Ground with regularity are the ones who hold onto their disappointment with tenacity. You must begin to challenge the despair, regret or disappointment around your marriage and your attachment to the ways you've failed one another. As a way to challenge what evil has done to your marriage, and will continue to do, you are to celebrate purposely the Common Ground you have tasted with your spouse. In doing this you are battling evil, who wants you to stay attached to the things that will weigh you down.

Your tendency is to forget the good things God does in your marriage by spending time and energy rehearsing the sin or evil that has been a part of your marriage. Instead, hold on to the good. As the Israelites were involved in the arduous task of rebuilding the Temple, the prophet Zechariah received a message from the Lord: "Do not despise these small beginnings, for the Lord rejoices just to see the work begin," (Zechariah 4:10). The best way to lean into the redemption the Lord brings into your life is to keep celebrating it, no matter how small it seems in comparison to the journey ahead. I have told the story of our sixteenth anniversary "Sisters in Motion" weekend over and over, and I'll keep telling it for the rest of my life. I don't ever plan on getting tired of talking about it.

THE TOGETHERNESS GOD CREATES

I have found the qualities of relational togetherness described in Ecclesiastes are a good reflection of the Common Ground you and your spouse are to celebrate together. "Two people can accomplish more than twice as much as one; they get a better return for their labor," (Ecclesiastes 4:9). Dawn and I spent many years trying to live in unity. To us, that meant we had to agree on everything and become more like one another. I tried to get her to approach life just like I did, and she did the same. We didn't realize we were stifling each other's gifts.

With more maturity I am able to encourage her gifts even though there are moments I still trip over them. However difficult it has been at times, living in the midst of her gifts has invited me to laugh, relax and relate with more sensitivity, which has complimented my strengths and transformed me into a more fruitful man. It's no different for Dawn. She approaches life with more intentionality and moves through relational difficulty with more confidence. This has only enhanced her gregarious and engaging personality. With a deeper love we give each other more permission to be different, without thinking that those differences threaten our togetherness. We find striving for unity to be stifling, while living in harmony is considerably more abundant. As we look back through the years it becomes easier and easier to see how we have helped shape each other in healthy ways. Being less threatened by our differences, while becoming more supportive of each other's strengths, has made us a much better team.

> With a deeper love, we give each other more permission to be different, without thinking that those differences threaten our togetherness.

In addition to celebrating increased fruitfulness, we are grateful that God's involvement in our marriage continues to make Dawn and me more graceful people. "If one person falls, the other can reach out and help. But people who are alone when they fall are in real trouble," (Ecclesiastes 4:10). I've come to realize how much I used to resent and pounce on Dawn's faults without realizing it. I didn't want her to have weaknesses, because I didn't really want to learn how to help her. I didn't want marriage to require something of me; I wanted it to give me something. The difficulty of marriage exposes a person's deep selfishness in such a way that God's grace and mercy become daily staples. If you feed on God's grace and mercy on a regular basis, you have more of it to give others. Because Dawn and I needed so much grace from God to stay at marriage, we had more grace for each other. Over time, our marriage became a place where tastes of undeserved kindness were not foreign. More and more, if one of us falls, the other reaches out to help.

As a couple softens and works together, their experience of sensual pleasure is heightened. There is warmth that comes just from being together. "And on a cold night, two under the same blanket can gain warmth from each other. But how can one be warm alone?" (Ecclesiastes 4:11). Pleasure, warmth, and connectedness are meant to help you remember God and His kindness. When you are fleshly and selfish, you ravage pleasure, trying to make a god out of it. As you soften and rest in God's commitment to you, you begin to trust that He will keep bringing you pleasure along the way. You no longer have to pillage it, but can drink it in and enjoy it.

Every good thing you receive is a gift from God (James 1:17). God wants to give you gifts as a way to endure the fallen-ness of this world. As marriage helps you grow humility and accept that all of life is a gift from God, you will begin to understand that sensual pleasure is a kindness that helps you endure. It is a foretaste of future glory. Marriage is one of God's most redemptive tools. When a couple follows God up the mountain, He will take them through the process of breaking up their flesh so that they are more receptive to His kindness and less reliant on their own strength. As this softening occurs, a couple's togetherness brings more warmth and sensual pleasure. This is a gift to celebrate.

Finally, in a marriage of Common Ground, each spouse is freer to battle sacrificially for the other. They can walk together and fight evil for the other instead of letting evil divide them. "A person standing alone can be attacked and defeated, but two can stand back-to-back and conquer," (Ecclesiastes 4:12). Marriage teaches you how to fight for another person against the things they can't even identify. As a single man, I could not see what was right in front of me, much less what was behind me. I was blind and unprotected when it came to disarming evil. I thought I could do it alone and unbeknownst to me, I didn't deeply trust the Lord or anyone else. Evil was robbing, killing and destroying, and I was oblivious to its reality.

Because marriage is so intimate, it awakens you to your blind spots. If you can learn to make room to soften and talk about your weaknesses, you can really begin to help one another. Dawn helps me to see what's right in front of me and as we soften together, she is learning how to help me deal with what I can't see – what is attacking me from behind. And when she does, she's prepared to fight evil for me. For example, I easily follow evil into workaholism. I see it a little better now, but Dawn sees it much more clearly. I need her to help me see and resist evil and this tendency to work too much. As we have grown in humility, each of us is more able to let the other help with the way evil attacks us personally. I now have more of a passion to come alongside her and help her to stand against evil, regardless of the reason she needs help. In some real ways I stand in the gap for her against evil, especially when she can't see him coming. He is not as free to bully and harass her.

Increased fruitfulness, more abundant grace, richer sensual pleasure, and the freedom to fight evil for each other are all gifts to keep celebrating as a couple growing in Common Ground. There are days and seasons were Dawn and I live in the richness of those qualities. There are also days and seasons that we don't. Our joy is that the seasons where those qualities are alive in our marriage are more regular, and we now trust they will keep coming all of our days.

> More and more, when one of us falls, the other reaches out to help.

The passage in Ecclesiastes ends this way: "Three are even better, for a triple-braided cord is not easily broken," (4:12B). *A triple-braided cord is not easily broken.* More than two decades after vowing to Dawn that I would love her like Christ did the Church, I have realized something. Evil is not that big and he is not that strong. God is the mighty warrior. As Dawn and I have stumbled into following Him better, letting Him fight for us, and receiving His gift of Common Ground, we are more convinced of His love and power. We have never deserved our moments of Common Ground and we won't deserve them any more in our future. But they will come, because God is big, and kind, and strong. *A triple-braided cord is not easily broken.* I know now He holds us and He won't let go.

"Then God will be given glory in everything through Jesus Christ.
All glory and power belong to him forever and ever. Amen."
(1 Peter 4:11)

ACKNOWLEDGEMENTS

So much of this book has been brought to life through my work at Daymark Pastoral Counseling. I am deeply grateful to the board members who have cared for and guided the ministry, to the supporters who have prayed for it and given financially, and to the many couples and individuals who have humbly opened their marriages to me, looking for help. In addition, many churches in Birmingham and the surrounding area have trusted me to provide counseling and teaching while they have also supported Daymark financially. Highest on this list is Oak Mountain Church and Bob Flayhart, who have been indescribably encouraging of my work. To all of you who have supported and believed in my work through Daymark Pastoral Counseling: You are a large part of this book.

I am especially indebted to Larry Crabb and Dan Allender. The time I spent studying under them remains the most formative and nourishing experience of my life in terms of my understanding of marriage and the Christian life. I can't imagine that there is much in these pages that did not originate with one or the other of them.

Thanks to Lauren Brooks, who spent a good five months working through the early inklings of a manuscript. Many of her comments and insights have become a valuable part of this work.

I am still shaking my head in disbelief at receiving back a manuscript half the size of the original, only to find it more engaging and better organized while retaining all the key ideas. How this was all done and still crafted in my words was simply a work of art. Thank you, Jodi MacNeal, for bringing your giftedness, hard work, deep concern and immeasurable skills to this project. You brought life to these words while also making them much more understandable to the reader.

My three girls – Aimee, Abby and Elise – love and encourage their Dad so well. Loving them is a treasure beyond surprise that has undone me in beautiful ways. The Lord has worked through them to soften and expand my heart more than I can describe. Their impact is interspersed throughout this book. Thank you, girls, for living life with passion and being such a gift to your Dad.

I couldn't begin to capture what Dawn has sacrificed to help birth the words in this book. I am reminded each morning that God's mercies are new when I get to see her face. The level of gratefulness I feel toward her is blinding. Her love is so undeserved and she has given me so much. If I have learned anything about marital love, it is because she has shared in it with me. Thank you for walking with me and helping me laugh. We have much to celebrate.

My gratefulness would not be complete without thanking the Lord. Your goodness gives all of this birth. In You I live and move and have my being. In whatever way the words in this book help others to see and know You better, I will be most grateful.

Gordon C. Bals
October 2012

SOURCES

Chapter 1: Common Ground: What Is It, and Where Do We Find It?

1.   Mike Mason, *The Mystery of Marriage: Meditations on the Miracle*, (Sisters, OR: Multnomah, 1985), 23.

Chapter 2: Evil: Not Everybody's Happy About Your Marriage

1.   Robert E. Webber, *Who Gets to Narrate the World? Contending for the Christian Story in an Age of Rivals*, (Downers Grove, IL: InterVarsity, 2008), 29.
2.   Clinton E. Arnold, *3 Crucial Questions about Spiritual Warfare*, (Grand Rapids, MI: Baker, 1997), 32.
3.   Kris Lundgaard, *The Enemy Within: Straight Talk About the Power and Defeat of Sin*, (Phillipsburg, NJ: P & R, 1998), 48.
4.   Dr. Fred Luskin, *Forgive for Love: The Missing Ingredient for a Healthy and Lasting Relationship*, (New York: HarperOne, 2007), 6.

Chapter 3: Cracking The Enemy's Code

1.   Mason, 46.
2.   C.S. Lewis, *The Four Loves*, (New York: Harcourt, 1960), 121-122.
3.   John Welwood, *Journey of the Heart: The Path of Conscious Love*, (Harper Perennial, 1990), 75.
4.   David Powlison, *Power Encounters: Reclaiming Spiritual Warfare*, (Grand Rapids, MI: Baker, 1995), 36.

Chapter 5: Adam & Eve Were Just Like Us

1.   Dan Allender and Tremper Longman, *Intimate Allies: Rediscovering God's Design for Marriage and Becoming Soul Mates for Life*, (Wheaton, IL: Tyndale House, 1995), 144.

Chapter 6: His Gifts, Her Gifts

1. Winston Smith, "Dichotomy or Trichotomy? How the Doctrine of Man Shapes the Treatment of Depression," *The Journal of Biblical Counseling,* 18.3, (Spring 2000): 24.
2. C. S. Lewis, *The Weight of Glory and Other Addresses,* (New York: Macmillan, 1949), 16.

Chapter 8: Defiant Humility

1. Carolyn Custis James, *The Gospel of Ruth: Loving God Enough to Break the Rules,* (Grand Rapids, MI: Zondervan, 2008), 102.
2. James, 103.
3. James, 102.

Chapter 13: Winsomeness

1. Larry Crabb, *Men and Women: Enjoying the Difference,* (Grand Rapids, MI: Zondervan, 1991), 199.

Chapter 14: Other-Centered Encouragement

1. Sharon Hersh, "The Desperation of God," *Mars Hill Review,* (Fall 1997): 26-27.

ABOUT THE AUTHORS

The first time Gordon Bals and Jodi (Davis) MacNeal appeared together in a photograph, they were 5 years old and standing with the rest of their classmates in their kindergarten class picture. Friendly rivals throughout their school days, they graduated from Manasquan (N.J.) High School and went their separate ways for more than 25 years, until God called them together to work on this book.

Dr. Gordon C. Bals, Ed.D., is the founder of Daymark Pastoral Counseling in Birmingham, Alabama. As a pastoral counselor who works with married couples from a variety of Christian communities, he has more than two decades of experience with everyday marital conflicts and has gained insight and wisdom on guiding couples toward togetherness. He is a sought-after speaker on topics as wide-ranging as marriage, parenting, grace, and building community. He has a doctorate in Pastoral Community Counseling from the University of Sarasota and a master's degree in Biblical Counseling from Colorado Christian University.

Other than counseling and teaching, Gordon likes to spend time with his wife and three daughters, and stays active by running, cycling and playing golf. He lives with his family in Homewood, Alabama, and has become absorbed in the South's real religion – college football.

Jodi MacNeal has spent more than 25 years looking after words – writing them, editing them, stringing them together in ways that inspire people to do (or feel) something special. An award-winning journalist and page designer, she has worked as a freelance writer, editor and creative consultant since 1998. She has edited a number of books, both fiction and non-fiction, and passionately pursues ministry communications as one of the ways she honors the Lord.

An accomplished speaker, Jodi also serves in the Southeast Florida Emmaus Community and volunteers as a school writing coach. She plays baseball, football, basketball, golf and tennis with her son, and also loves to read, cook and hike. Jodi's husband, Alan, passed away in 2004. She lives in Florida with their son, Joshua.

Visit her at www.jodimacneal.com.

ABOUT DAYMARK PASTORAL COUNSELING

Daymark Pastoral Counseling is a non-profit counseling and teaching agency. Through it, we seek to reflect the light of the Gospel and the counsel of Scripture to assist believers toward depth, maturity and restoration of relationship with God and with one another. Its counselors work on a sliding scale based on clients' income. In addition to seminars and workshops based on the material from *Common Ground*, Dr. Gordon Bals does a variety of other presentations to assist churches or Christian organizations. Audio versions of his seminars (including *Common Ground*) and other teachings are available for purchase.

Learn more at www.daymarkcounseling.com.

Made in the USA
Charleston, SC
09 May 2014